Historic Canada

HALIFAX
SOUTH END

Historic
Canada

HALIFAX
SOUTH END

James Cornall

ARCADIA
PUBLISHING

ISBN 978-0-7385-7272-7

Published by Arcadia Publishing
Charleston SC, Chicago IL, Portsmouth NH, San Francisco CA

Printed in the United States of America

Library of Congress Catalog Card Number: 2009936604

For all general information contact Arcadia Publishing at:
Telephone 843-853-2070
Fax 843-853-0044
E-mail sales@arcadiapublishing.com
For customer service and orders:
Toll-Free 1-888-313-2665

Visit us on the Internet at www.arcadiapublishing.com

Contents

ACKNOWLEDGMENTS

I would like to thank the following for their assistance in the production of this book: Angela Cornall, John and Jean Cornall, Avon and Myrna Bayers, Garry Shutlak at the Public Archives of Nova Scotia for his assistance and knowledge, and the photographers both known and unknown who unwittingly made history so tangible.

This book is dedicated to the memory of Mary Doreen Chapman (nee Smith), who always saw the beauty in everything and everyone.

Bibliography

Akins, Dr. Thomas B. *History of Halifax City*, 1895.
Payzant, *Joan M. Halifax Cornerstone of Canada Windsor Publications, Inc.*, 1985.
Raddall, Thomas H. *Halifax, Warden of the North McClelland and Stewart*, 1971.

INTRODUCTION

Exactly when European settlers first set eyes upon North America has long been debated. What is for certain, however, is that the first settlers to come across Chebooktook, as the native peoples called it, were entering into the second largest natural harbour in the world, a land of tree-covered hills, and fish-filled waters.

As the French and English began to settle different parts of Nova Scotia, Chebooktook became Chebucto. On June 21, 1749, Edward Cornwallis changed the name to Halifax, honouring his patron, the president of the English Board of Trade and Plantations, the Earl of Halifax, otherwise known as George Dunk. It was also in 1749 that Halifax became capital of the Province of Nova Scotia, replacing Annapolis Royal.

Because of its location, Halifax was, and has continued to be of great importance in a military sense, with the lingering effects of conflicts between England and France, as well as the American War of Independence in 1776. Walking around the city today the strong connection to its military and naval history is apparent. Almost 250 years have passed since the beginning of the city, and since then Halifax has continued to grow, becoming the most important port in Canada, and becoming a "City of Firsts" along the way.

Canada's first Protestant church was erected in Halifax, and the first English newspaper was published there as well. The first zoo, first distillery, the first city in North America to be lit entirely by electricity in 1890, the first divorce court, and the first saltwater ferry service all are wrapped into the rich and long history of Halifax. In addition, Government House, first occupied by Gov. John Wentworth in 1807, is considered the oldest continually used official residence in North America.

Halifax can probably boast more events in its history than many cities in North America. The entire city was altered forever on December 6, 1917, when two ships, the *Imo* and the *Mont Blanc* collided in Halifax Harbour. People crowded around the harbour to watch, and small vessels rushed to the scene. Seventeen minutes after the collision, the biggest man-made explosion in history until Hiroshima occurred, killing two thousand and injuring two thousand more. Much of the North End of Halifax was completely destroyed.

Five years earlier, further establishing the connection between Halifax and the sea, the city played centre stage to the Titanic disaster of April 1912, with many of the bodies having been brought to Halifax. Because of its connections to military and naval history, and the obvious relationship with Great Britain, Halifax was a thriving city at the turn of the 20th century. Fortunately, excellent records exist from the earliest days of photography, giving a wonderful glimpse into life in the bustling port of Halifax. The photographs contained in this volume are mostly from the turn of the century, with some as old as 1865, and others as recent as 1920.

The new century brought a great deal of change. The city was heavily involved in the Boer War. Within a year, Queen Victoria would die, sending the entire British Empire into shock. The Titanic disaster, the First World War, and the Halifax Explosion changed the city yet more, and Canada's development as a country also pushed Halifax into new directions.

In this volume, the photographic history of the South End of Halifax is being presented. The City of Halifax has been divided arbitrarily over the years in many ways. Some consider Halifax to be sub-divided into North End, downtown, South End, and even the West End. Others split the city into two or three segments, using North and South Streets as boundary lines. Such divisions are man-made and often pointless.

For the purposes of this book, I have chosen a turn-of-the-century boundary (and extended it) which serves to neatly divide the city into two reasonably equal and distinct parts. Beginning at the Waterfront, the line heads down what was Hurd's Lane, then follows Cogswell Street to North Park, before heading down Cunard as far as Windsor Street. The imaginary line then follows Chebucto Road as far as the Northwest Arm, where the Armdale Rotary currently stands.

The measure of the history of a city should not be solely facts and events, but should include the everyday scenery that puts those events into perspective. May this book provide you with a taste of life in the South End of Halifax from the 1860s through to 1920—a period which encompasses three monarchs, two wars, and one great city.

One

PANORAMAS

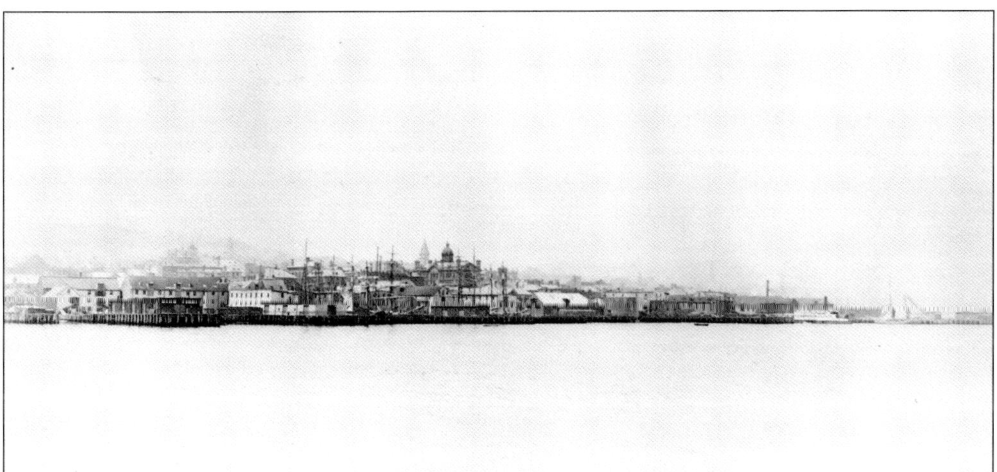

This is turn-of-the-century Halifax as seen from George's Island (Courtesy of the Photograph Collection, Public Archives of Nova Scotia, Notman Collection, #67513.)

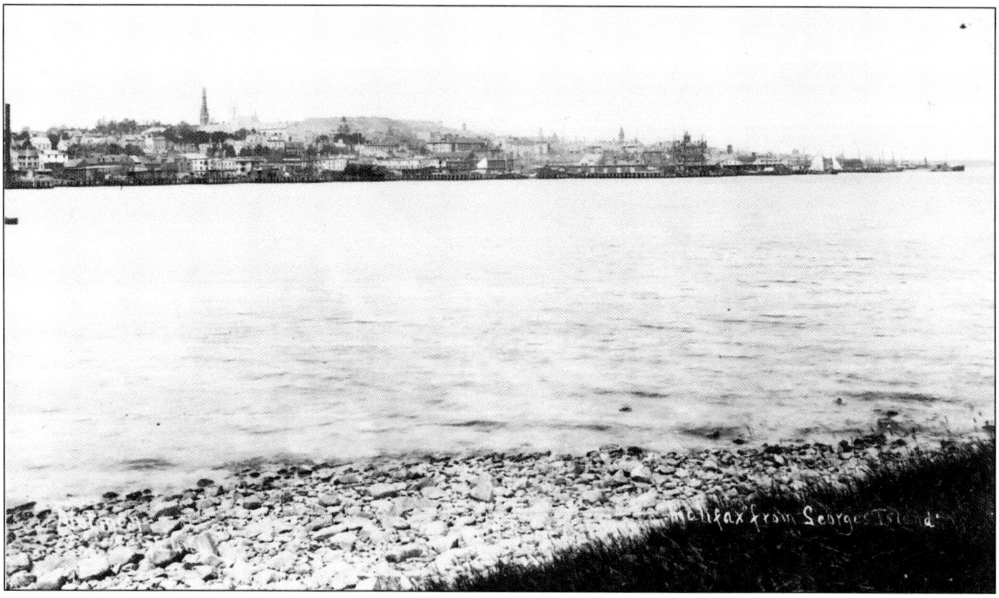

The view of Halifax for those entering the harbour has always been a spectacular one. One of the best vantage points for photographers has always been George's Island, which sits in the middle of Halifax Harbour. This c. 1910 photograph shows much of downtown, including the Academy of Music, John McInnes and Co. Lumber Warehouse, city hall, Province House, and St. Mary's Roman Catholic Cathedral. (Courtesy of the Photograph Collection, Public Archives of Nova Scotia, Notman Collection, #72444.)

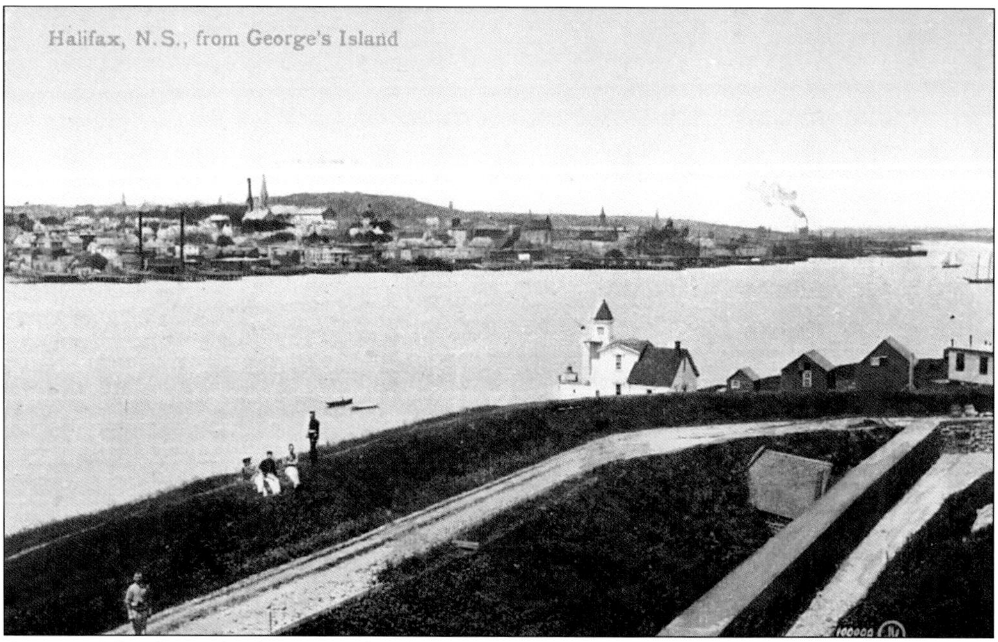

George's Island was the first part of Halifax to be fortified. Although the island was not strictly part of the South End, this postcard from the early 1900s shows the proximity of the island and the sparse downtown with Citadel Hill dominating the skyline. On old French maps, the island was known as Isle Racket or Snowshoe Island because of its shape.

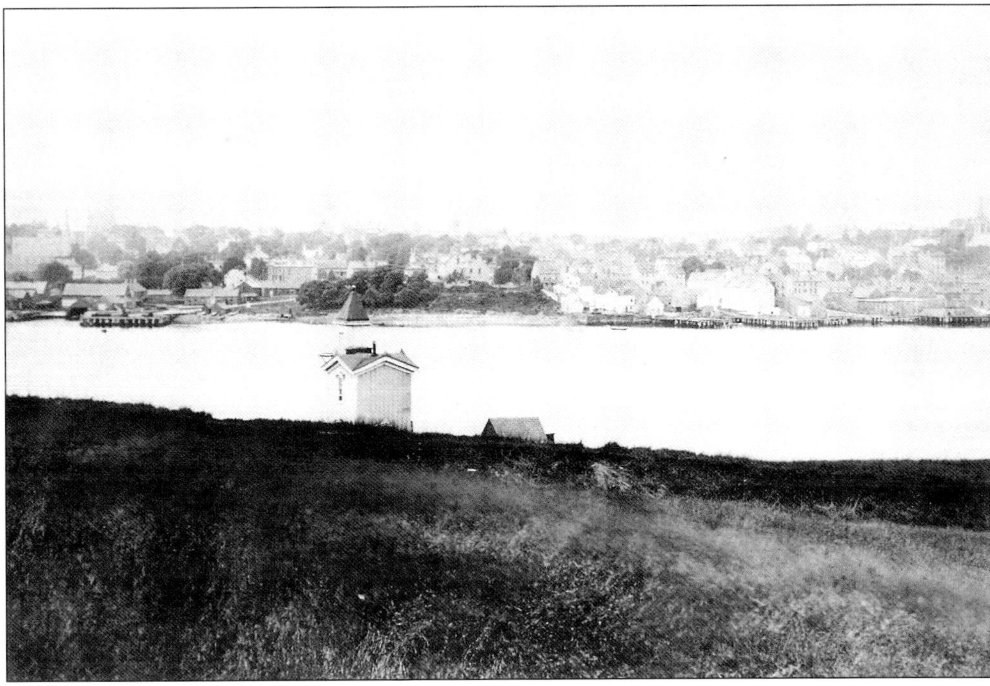

This early image of the Halifax downtown, c. 1875 was taken on George's Island. A number of wharves can clearly be seen, as can the Town Clock on Citadel Hill in the centre of the picture. (Courtesy of the Photograph Collection, Public Archives of Nova Scotia, Halifax General View 5 : PANS N-1367.)

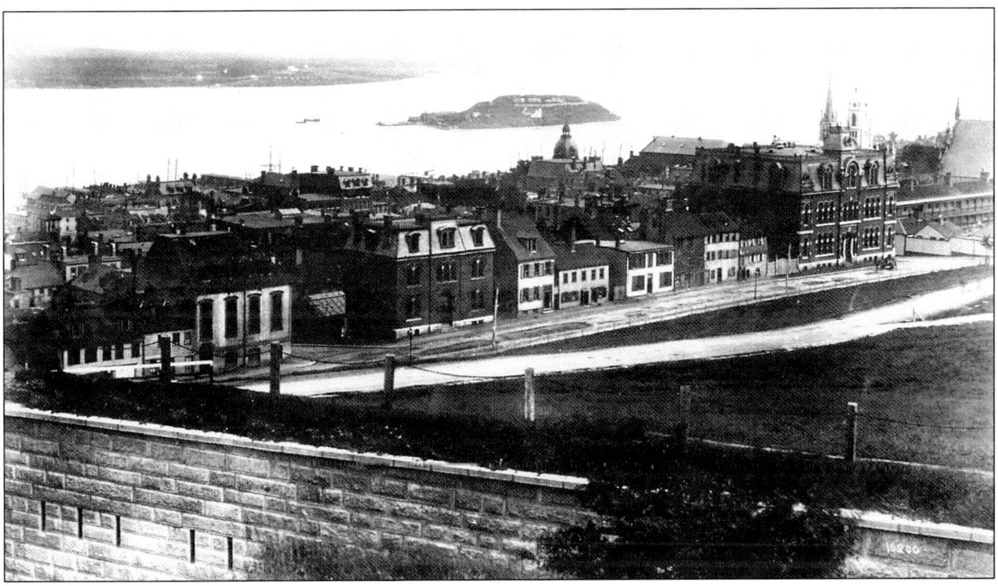

Looking in the opposite direction, from the Citadel out towards the harbour, George's Island takes centre stage in this 1884 view. To the right is McNab's Island, and on the opposite shore, Eastern Passage. A horse and cart can be seen wending its way along Brunswick Street. (Courtesy of the Photograph Collection, Public Archives of Nova Scotia, Notman Collection #10200.)

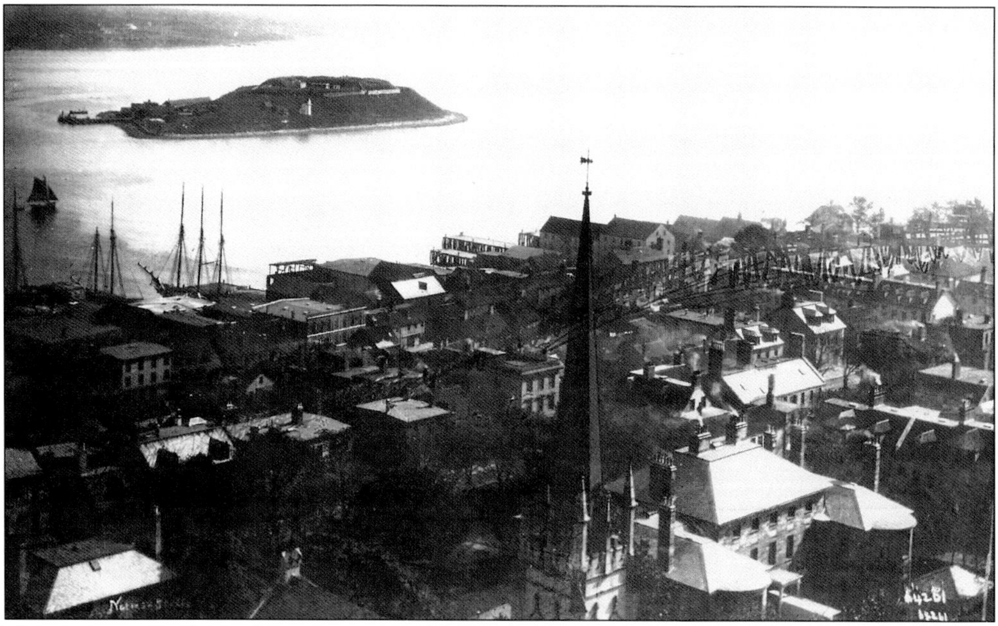

The entrance to the harbour is more visible on this 1888 photograph taken from high atop the spire of St. Mary's Cathedral. St. Matthew's spire dominates, and ships can be spotted along the wharves as can the fortified and treeless George's Island. (Courtesy of the Photograph Collection, Public Archives of Nova Scotia, Notman Collection, #64261.)

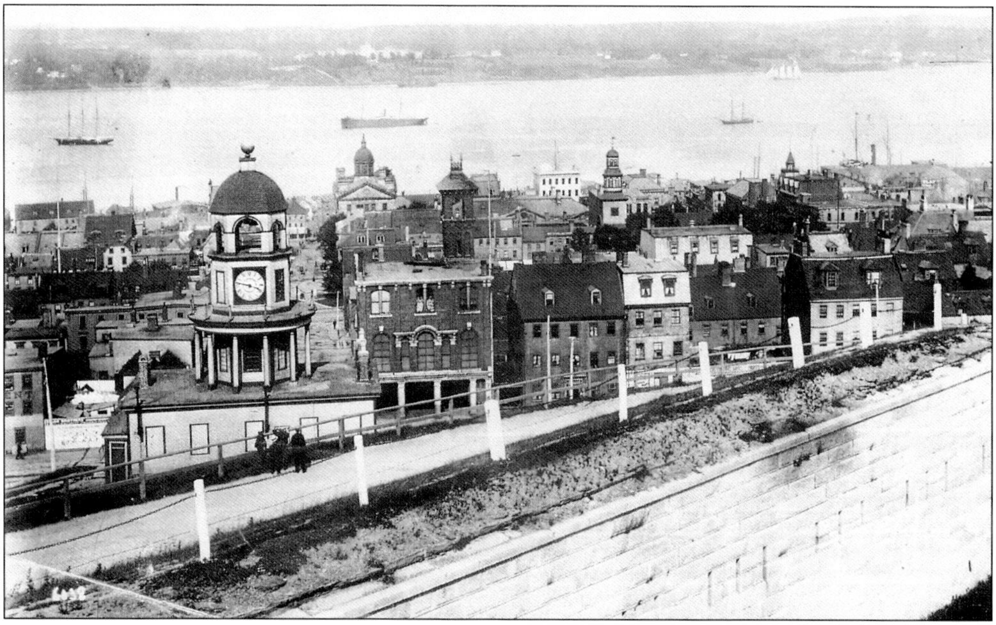

The downtown of Halifax as observed from Citadel Hill is what is seen in this 1890 picture. In front is the Old Town Clock that Edward, Duke of Kent, had installed in 1803 to ensure punctuality. Directly behind the Clock is George Street heading down to the waterfront, with its horse-drawn vehicles visible. On the corner of George Street and Brunswick Street is the Central Engine Station, with two ladies talking in the third floor windows! (Courtesy of the Photograph Collection, Public Archives of Nova Scotia, Notman Collection, #6038.)

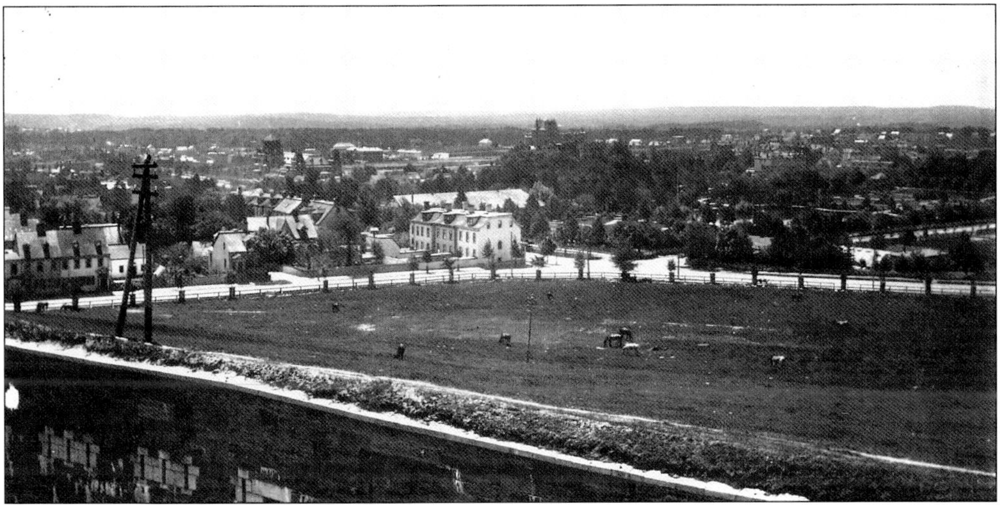

Looking southwest, from the opposite side of Citadel Hill, *c.* 1880, the already well-established 17-acre park of the Public Gardens can be seen, at the corner of Sackville and South Streets. The design of the Gardens as it stands today was undertaken by Richard Power in 1875. Much of the South End of Halifax is visible, as well. (Courtesy of the Photograph Collection, Public Archives of Nova Scotia, Notman Collection, #44223.)

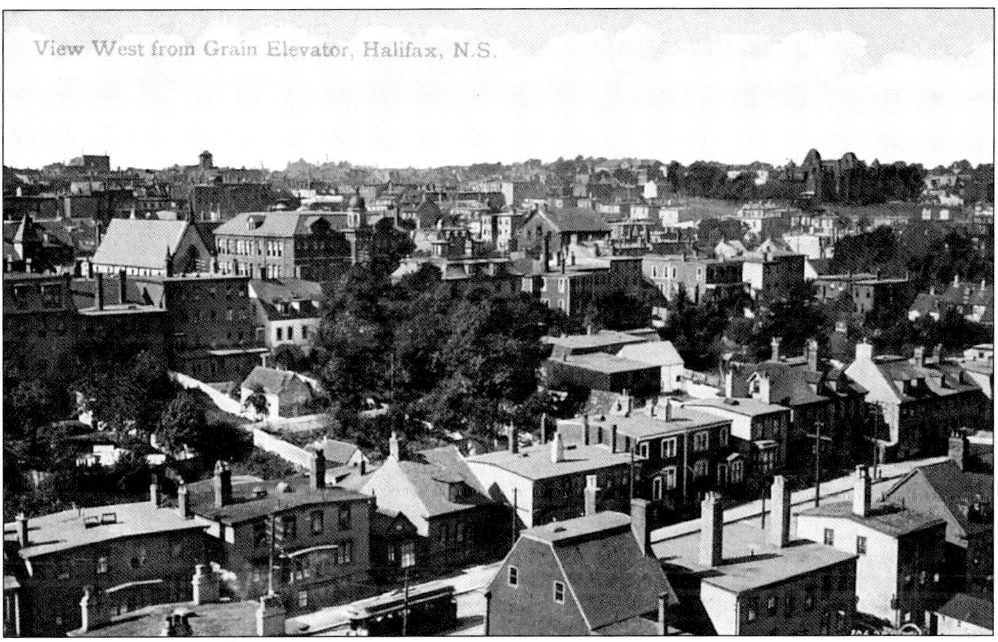

Deep in the South End of Halifax, along the waterfront, the Grain Elevator still stands. Along with Citadel Hill and the church spires, it provided a wonderful vista from which to photograph the South End and downtown. This western view, taken in the early 1900s, fortuitously shows a streetcar running along Barrington Street.

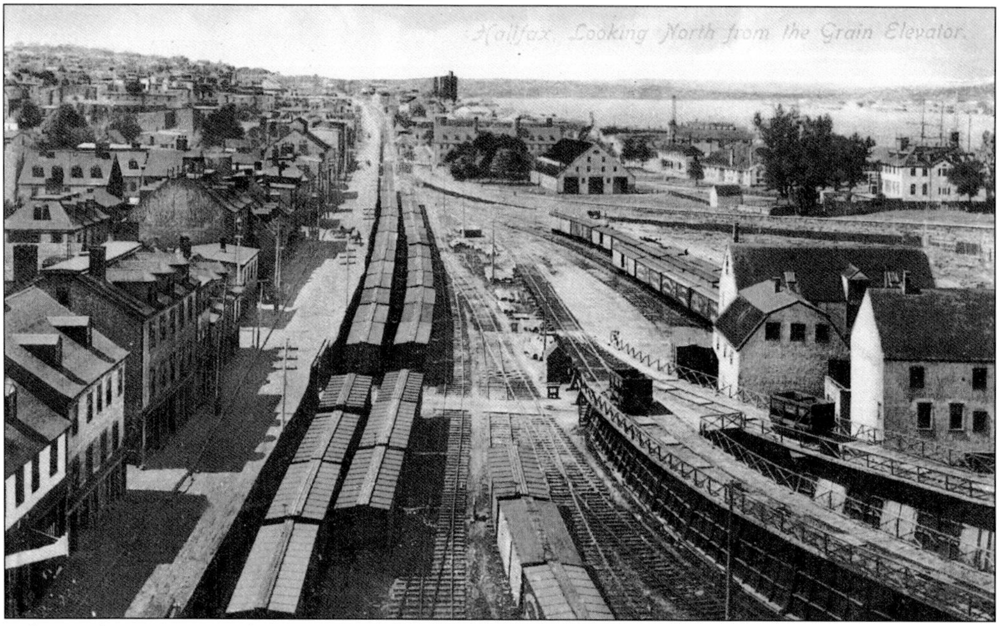

When taking pictures from any distinctive height, usually all four points of the compass are covered at the same time. This view north from the Grain Elevator shows the train tracks heading into the city to the ill-fated I.C.R. Station at the corner of Barrington and North Streets, which was destroyed in the 1917 Explosion.

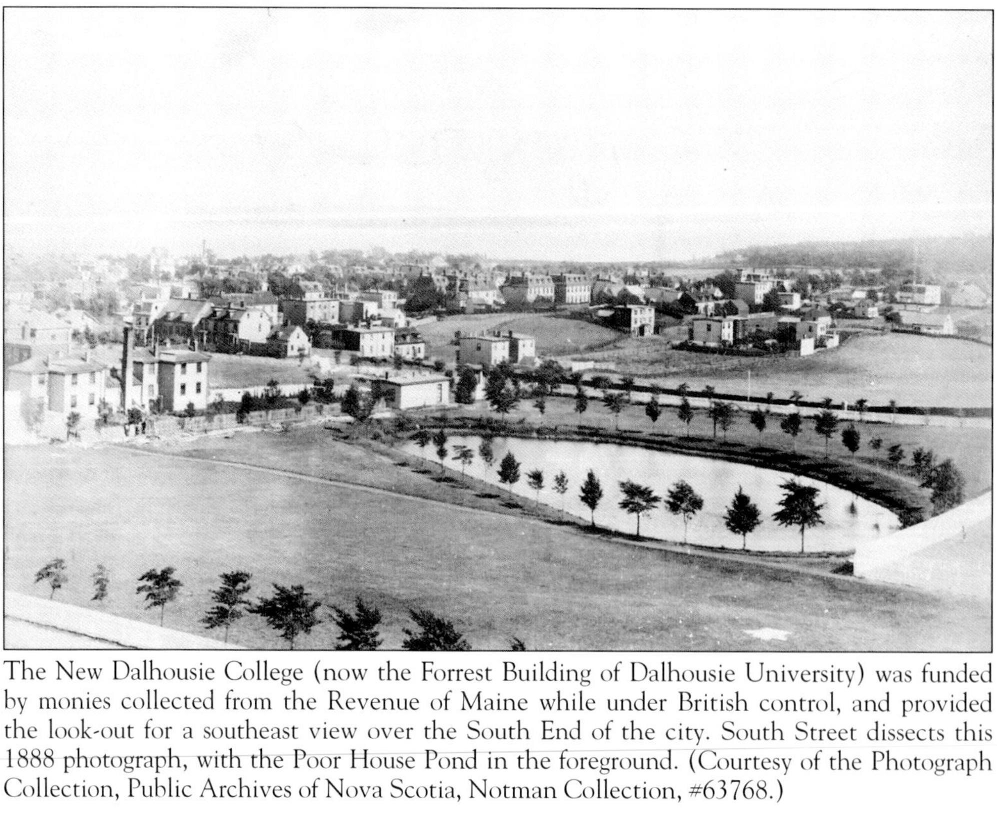

The New Dalhousie College (now the Forrest Building of Dalhousie University) was funded by monies collected from the Revenue of Maine while under British control, and provided the look-out for a southeast view over the South End of the city. South Street dissects this 1888 photograph, with the Poor House Pond in the foreground. (Courtesy of the Photograph Collection, Public Archives of Nova Scotia, Notman Collection, #63768.)

Two

Street Scenes

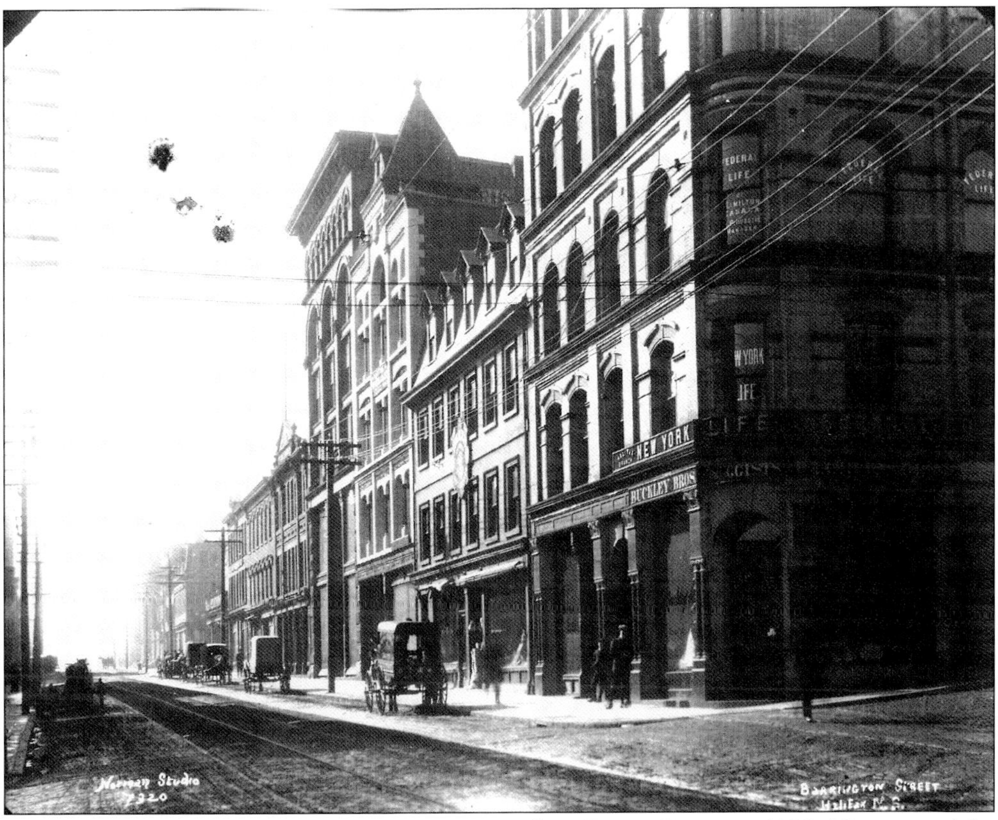

This is a view looking south on Barrington Street from Prince Street, *c.* 1900. (Courtesy of the Photograph Collection, Public Archives of Nova Scotia, Notman Collection, #7320.)

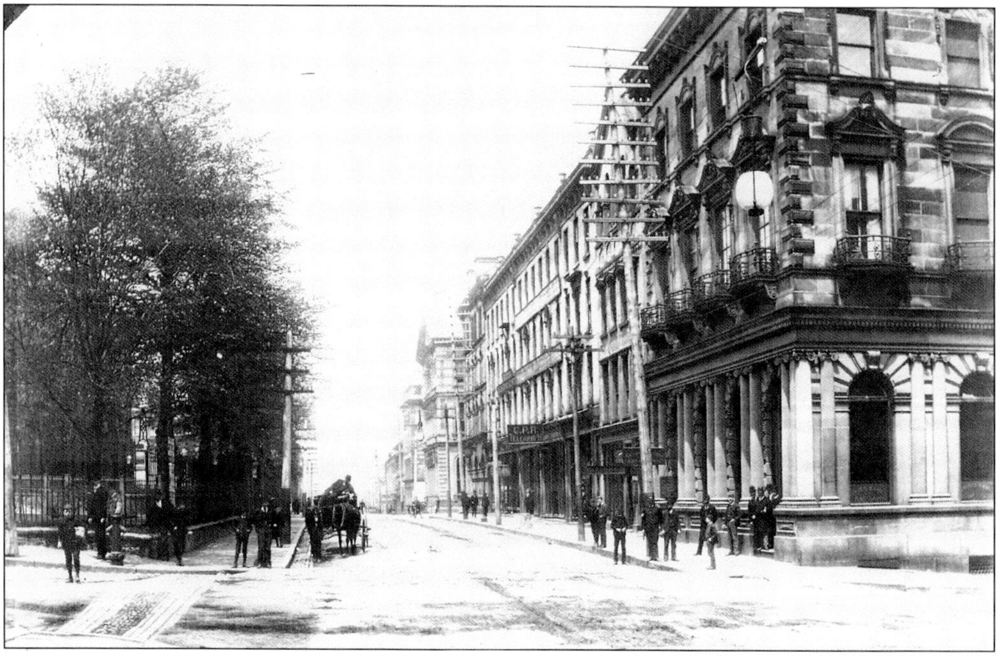

This photograph of Hollis Street facing north from Prince Street shows the Union Bank of Halifax in the foreground and the C.P.R. Telegraph office. (Courtesy of the Photograph Collection, Public Archives of Nova Scotia, Notman Collection, #69530.)

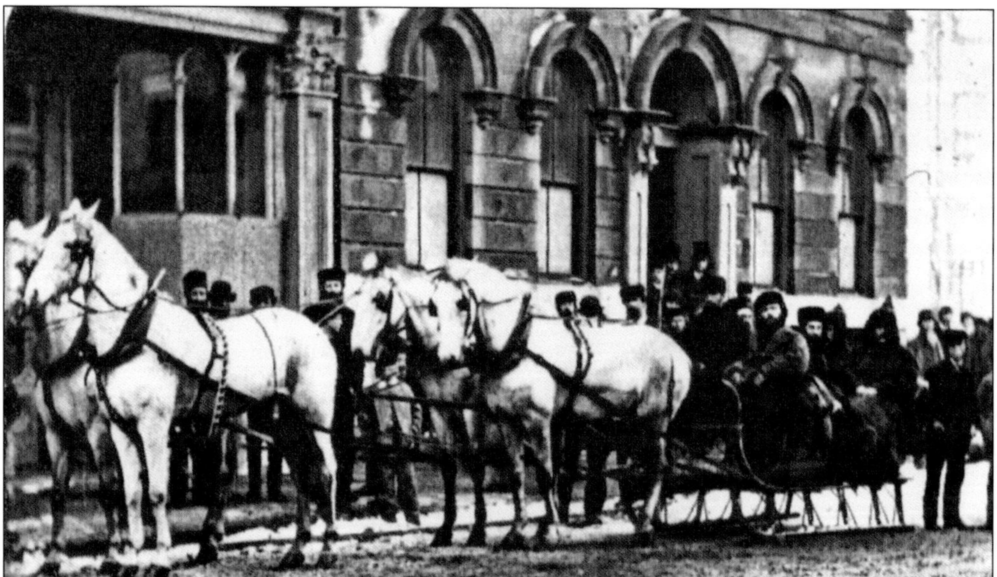

The horses and sled, with occupants in suitable winter attire, pose in front of the Doull & Miller Building at the corner of Hollis and Sackville Streets. A large portion of Hollis Street was destroyed by one of many fires in 1859. The lot was sold to Mr. Doull. Doull & Miller also bought a building at the corner of Hollis and Prince Streets in May of 1857 for the princely sum of £3,450. (Courtesy of the Photograph Collection, Public Archives of Nova Scotia, W. Chase Collection, Album #5, #61.)

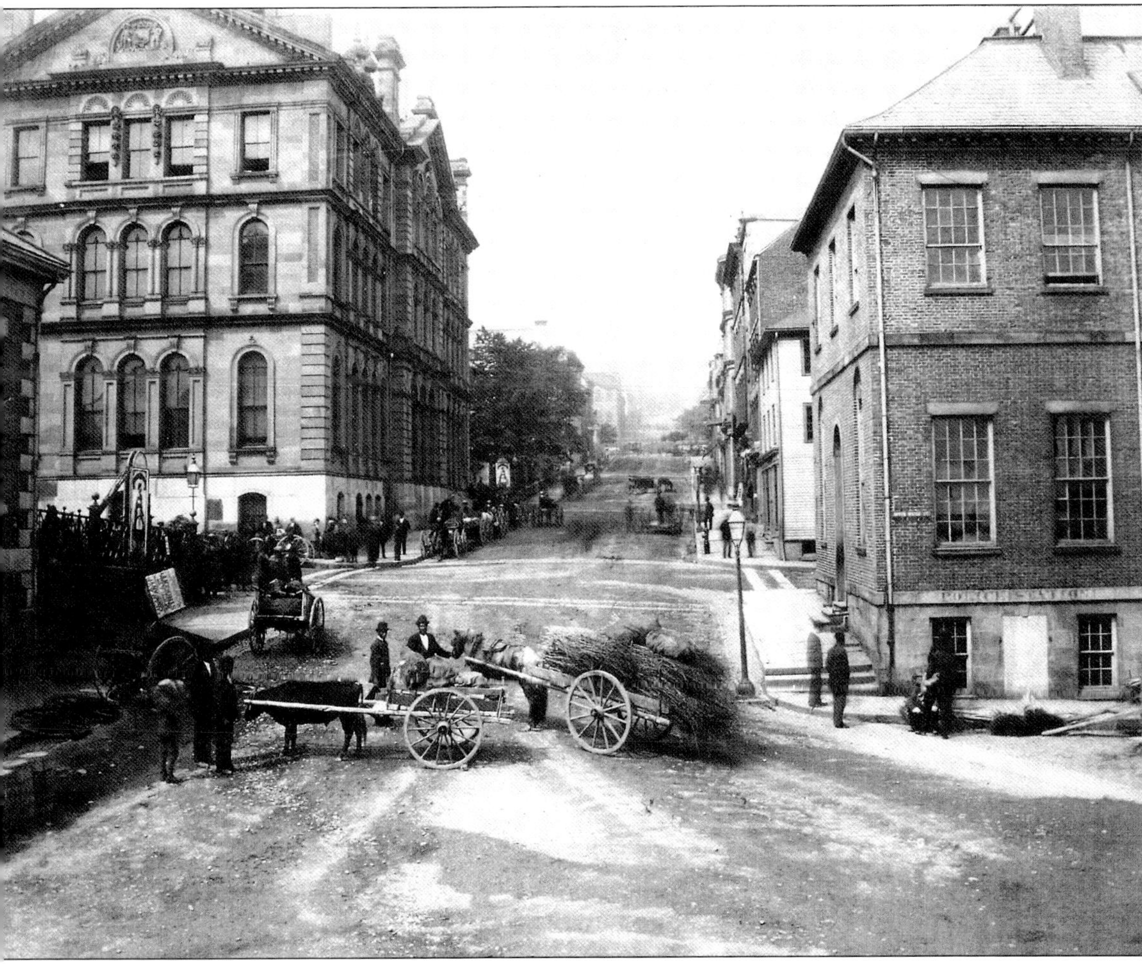

One of the busiest streets in downtown Halifax was always George Street, running from the Town Clock on Citadel Hill to Bedford Row by the waterfront. This view is taken from the foot of George Street looking up towards the clock, and was taken c. 1883. In the foreground to the right is the police station, and the large building to the left shows the post office and Custom House. The street sign on the police station showing Upper Water Street is clear, as is an advertisement for the Fifth Avenue Company and Michael Strogoff. In addition to the numerous horse-drawn carts, it is interesting to note an ox-drawn cart in the picture. (Courtesy of the Photograph Collection, Public Archives of Nova Scotia, Notman Collection, #44222.)

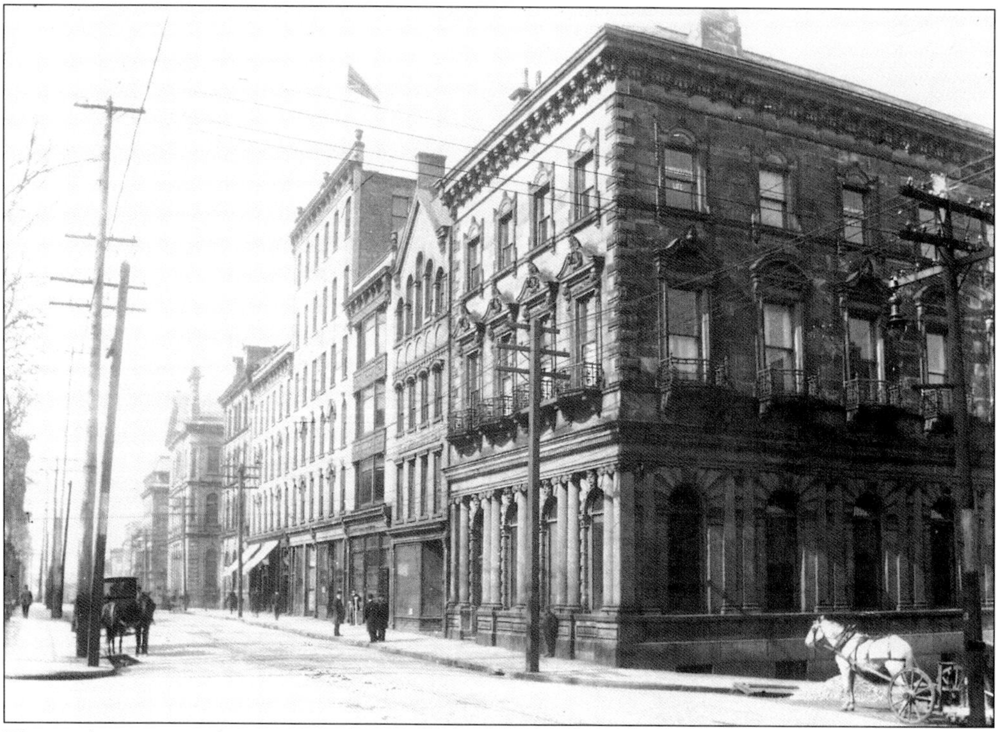

This is the corner of Prince and Hollis Streets *c.* 1913. The picture shows the T.B. McCurdy & Co. Building and the Metropole Building. Forty-five Hollis Street was named after Lady Grace Holles, the mother of British Prime Minister Henry Pelham, and, was primarily retail from Sackville to George Streets and residential at the south end. (Courtesy of the Photograph Collection, Public Archives of Nova Scotia, Notman Collection.)

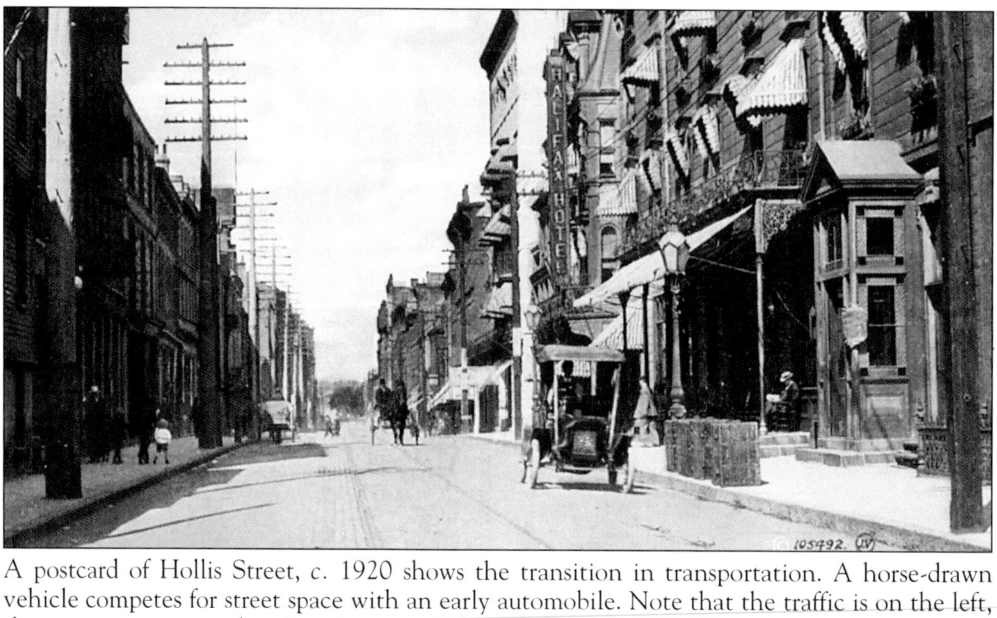

A postcard of Hollis Street, *c.* 1920 shows the transition in transportation. A horse-drawn vehicle competes for street space with an early automobile. Note that the traffic is on the left, the same system as used in Great Britain, and one that was maintained until later in the decade. The Queen and Halifax Hotels can also be seen.

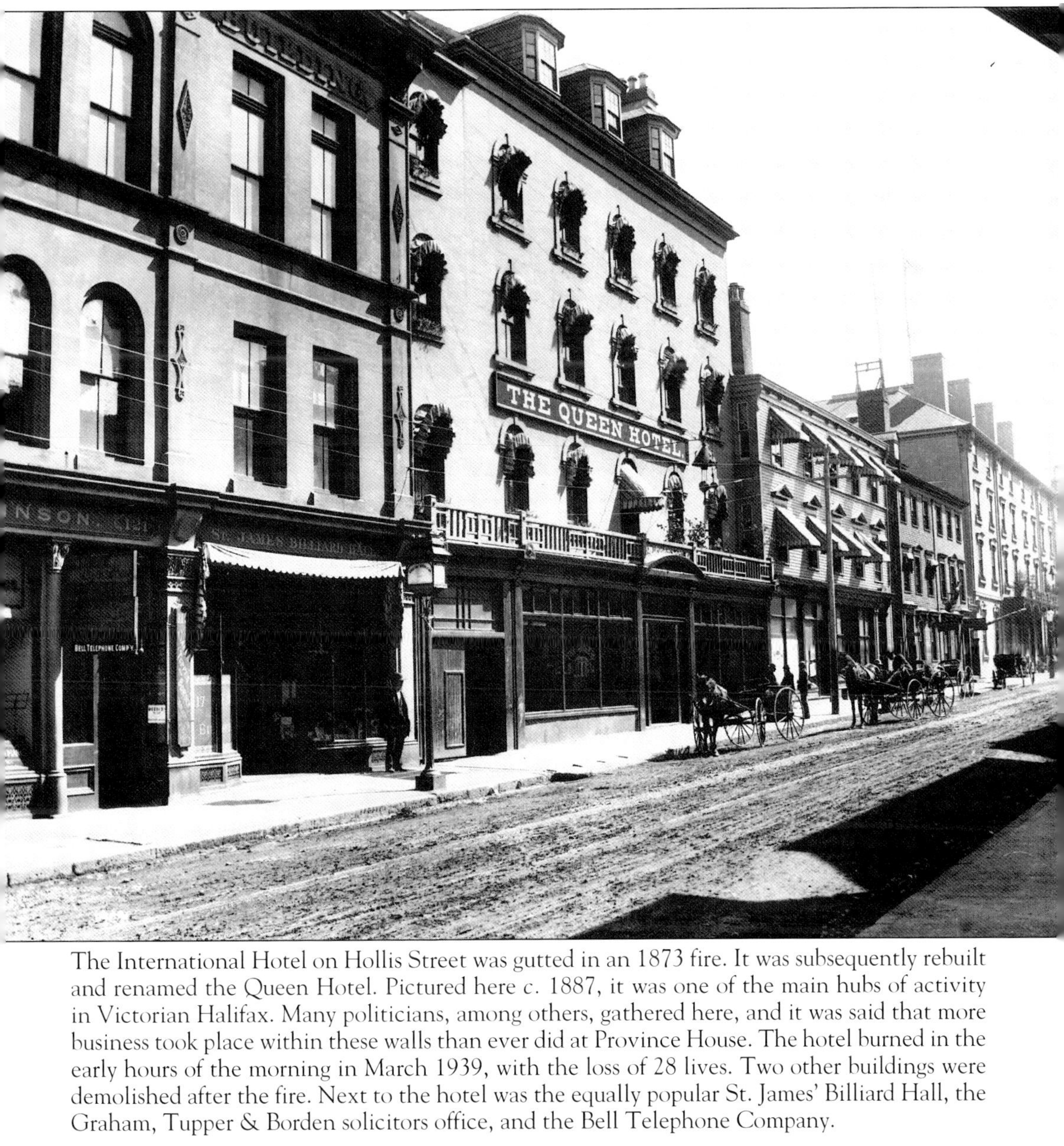

The International Hotel on Hollis Street was gutted in an 1873 fire. It was subsequently rebuilt and renamed the Queen Hotel. Pictured here c. 1887, it was one of the main hubs of activity in Victorian Halifax. Many politicians, among others, gathered here, and it was said that more business took place within these walls than ever did at Province House. The hotel burned in the early hours of the morning in March 1939, with the loss of 28 lives. Two other buildings were demolished after the fire. Next to the hotel was the equally popular St. James' Billiard Hall, the Graham, Tupper & Borden solicitors office, and the Bell Telephone Company.

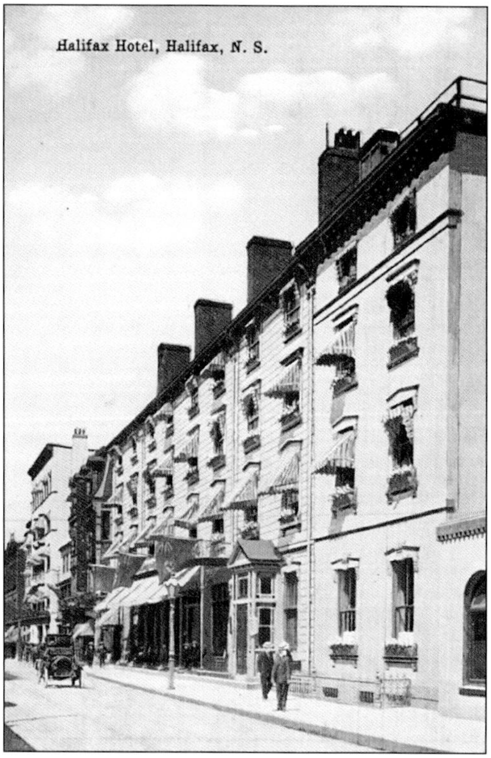

The Halifax Hotel, also on Hollis Street, opened in 1841, and quickly became the most exclusive hotel in the city. In 1851, it was leased to the Garrison at Halifax for three years. By 1893, it could accommodate 350 guests, and in 1897 became the first hotel in the province with an elevator. Like the Queen Hotel it also ceased to exist, not due to fire, but to bankruptcy, and closed May 14, 1943. It was demolished in 1948 to make way for a new Provincial Government annex. This postcard shows the hotel in its heyday, c. 1920.

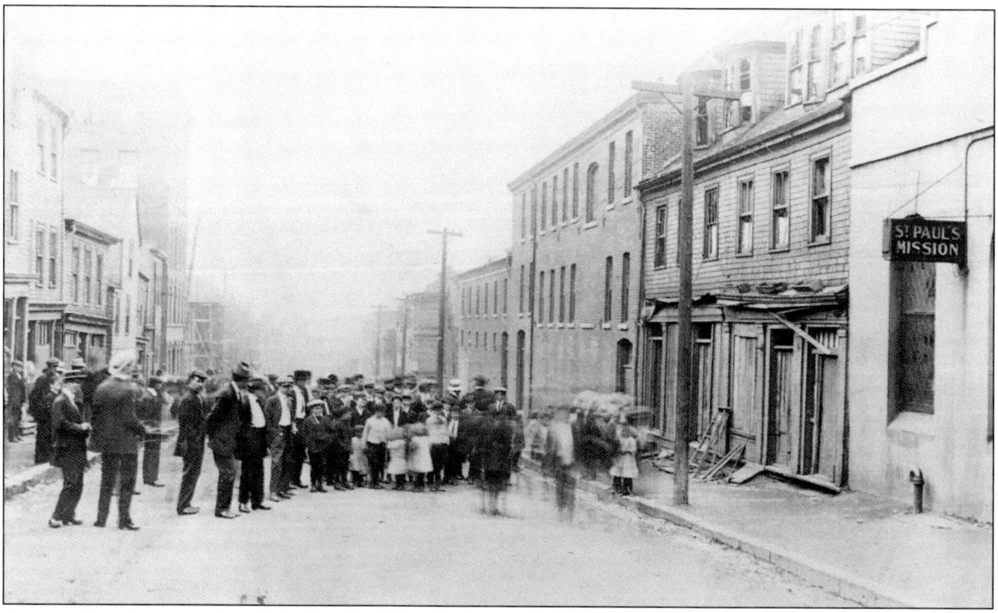

A crowd waits outside of St. Paul's Church Mission. This photograph from c. 1913 was taken along Albemarle Street, which subsequently changed its name to Market Street. St. Paul's Shelter was open to all regardless of religion, and provided free beds and meals to men returning to work after hospitalization or who were seeking employment. The St. Paul's Mission Hall had originally been the Old National School until 1896. (Courtesy of the Photograph Collection, Public Archives of Nova Scotia, Moirs Collection #14.)

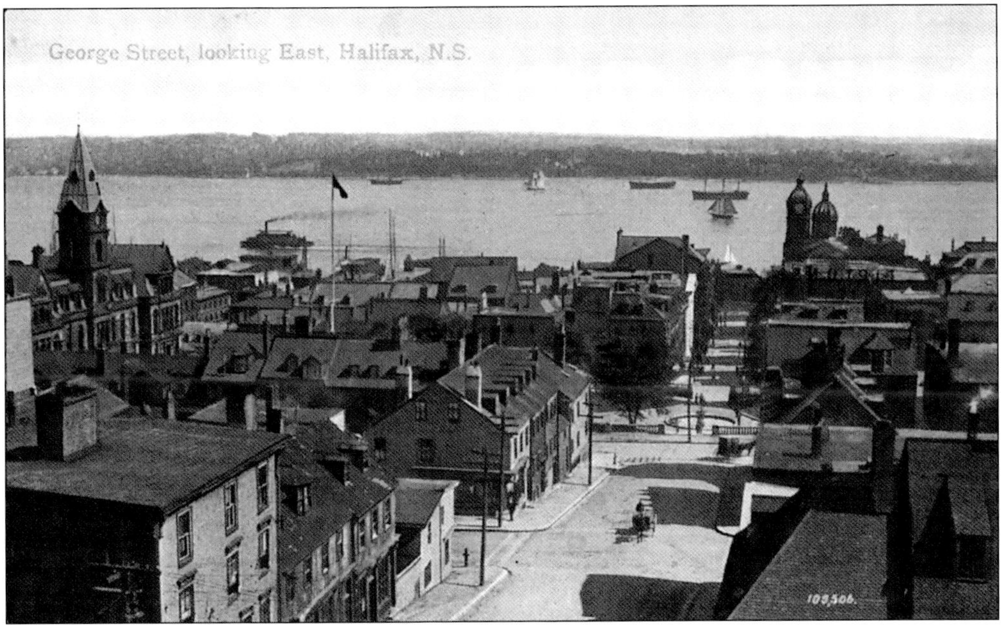

Taken from the foot of the Town Clock on Citadel Hill, this *c.* 1900 view along George Street shows the Custom House and post office, and the city hall on the left of the picture. Just below the post office an advertisement for Liptons Tea can be seen in reverse. In the harbour the Dartmouth to Halifax ferry takes its passengers between the two communities before bridges united them.

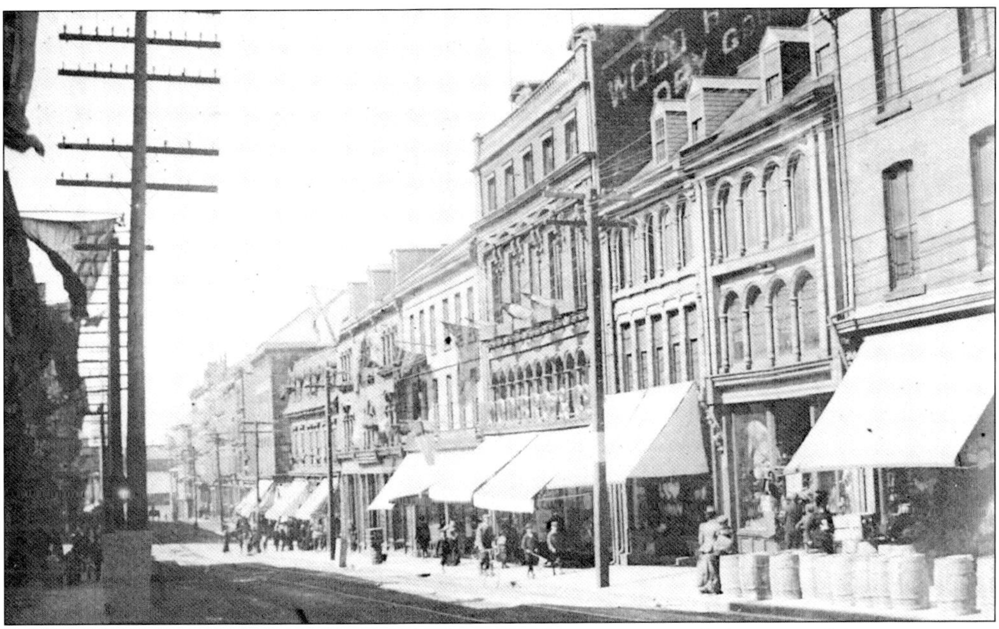

Another city street which was a hive of commercial activity around the turn of the century was Granville Street. Many storefronts can be seen here, including Wood Brothers Dry Goods store. The Union Flag flies proudly from the building, long before the current Canadian flag saw the light of day over half a century later. (Courtesy of the Photograph Collection, Public Archives of Nova Scotia, J.A. Irvine Collection, Album #36, #54.)

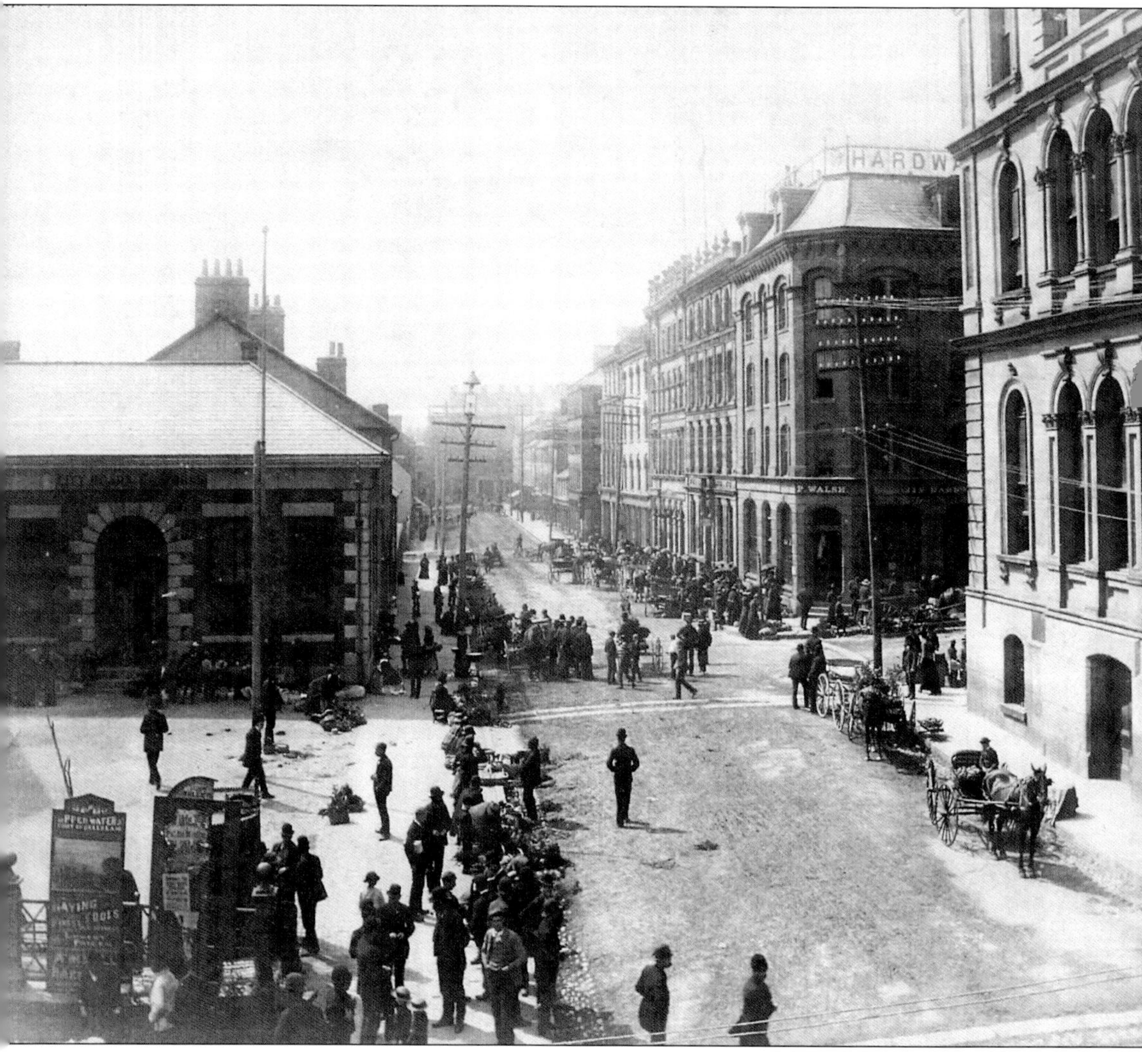

Market Day brought citizens from around the region to sell their wares, at the Bedford Row location of the market. The P. Walsh City Hardware can clearly be seen, and the building at the far right is the Cheapside Post Office. The building on the left of this *c.* 1890 photograph is the City Board of Works building, built as a market house in 1851. In the bottom left hand corner, advertisements for A.M. Bell's Hardware store and the Academy of Music bulletin board with various notices are apparent. Two cobblestone granite street crossings can be seen, as well as a cobblestone gutter. (Courtesy of the Photograph Collection, Public Archives of Nova Scotia, Notman Collection, #69577.)

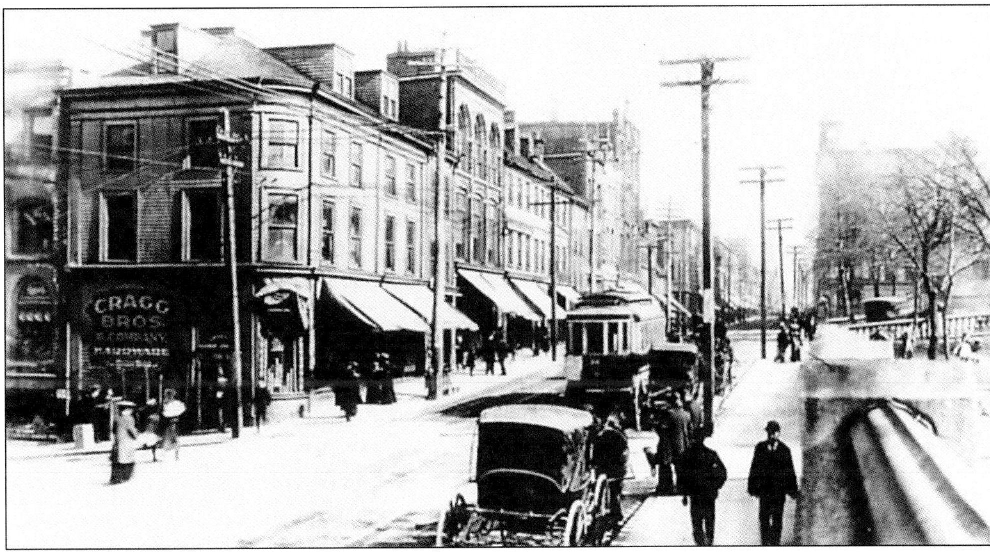

By contrast to the open cars, this beautiful photograph of a closed car, car #34, can be seen at the corner of George and Barrington Streets, outside of the busy Cragg Bros. Hardware Store. The first electric streetcar trundled along Barrington Street in February 1896. Just six years earlier, Halifax had become the first North American city to be lit entirely by electricity. (Courtesy of the Photograph Collection, Public Archives of Nova Scotia, Trans. & Com. Streetcars 1896–1908.)

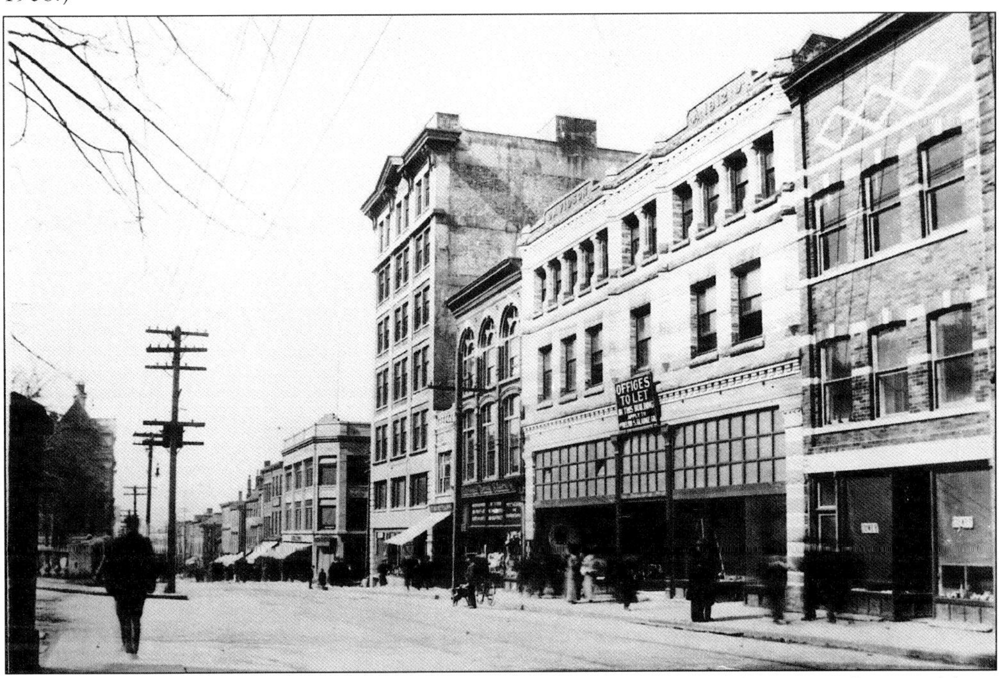

This c. 1913 picture shows Barrington Street facing north. The Clyde L. Davidson Building, stationers, is to the right, and advertises offices to let. Next door, a drugstore, Kinley's Ltd., does business. Also seen are H. Schaefer & Sons, Jeweler, and the Cragg (hardware) Building. While still an important thoroughfare, Barrington Street, named after British Statesman the Viscount Barrington of Ardyless, has changed emphasis with regards to commerce.

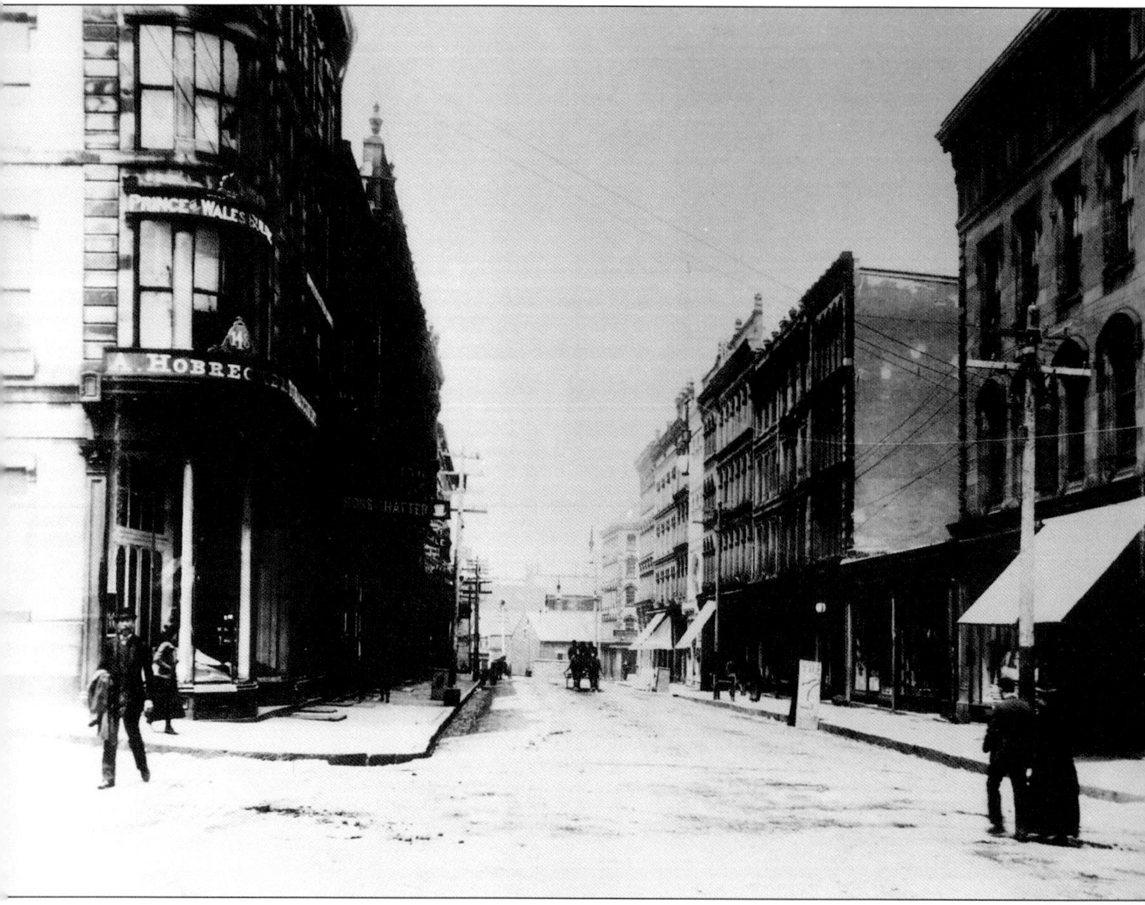

In 1859, a million dollars worth of damage, a colossal amount of money for the day, was done by a fire that devastated the area. By 1890, when this photograph was taken, the "Granville Street" fire was all but forgotten. This picture, looking north along the street to the intersection of Water and Buckingham Streets, shows many storefronts, such as Ross, Hatters, and A. Hobrecher, Tobacconist, in the Prince of Wales Building. Store boards also line the gutter, and calmly ambling along the road was of little danger. (Courtesy of the Photograph Collection, Public Archives of Nova Scotia, Notman Collection, #64529.)

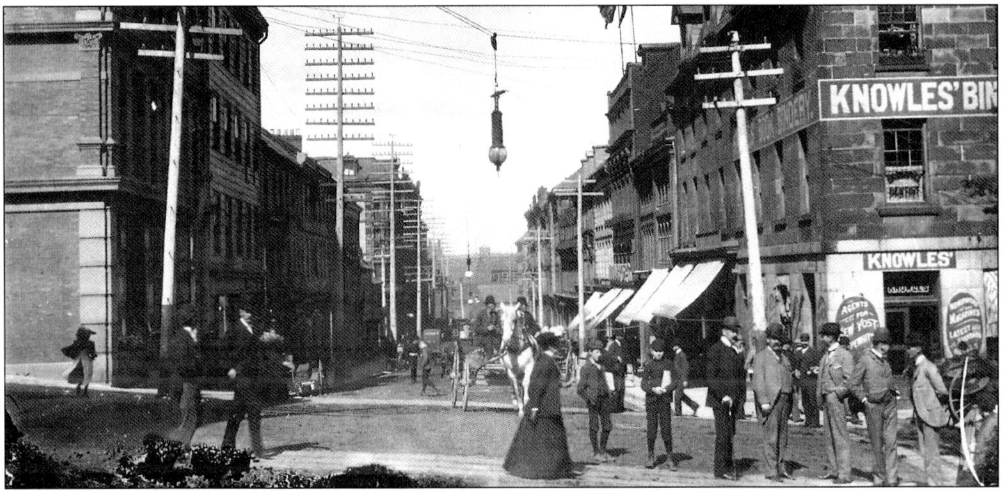

A little farther along Granville Street, still facing north, is the George Street intersection c. 1894. Knowles Book Bindery at 95 Granville Street offers "Newspapers, Magazines, Latest and Standard Novels," as well as an advertisement for typewriters, one of the new-fangled consumer items one could purchase in the years leading up to the new century. A dentist's office graces the room above. At 110 Granville Street, W.H. Newman, Jewelers was located. (Courtesy of the Photograph Collection, Public Archives of Nova Scotia, Notman Collection, #2186.)

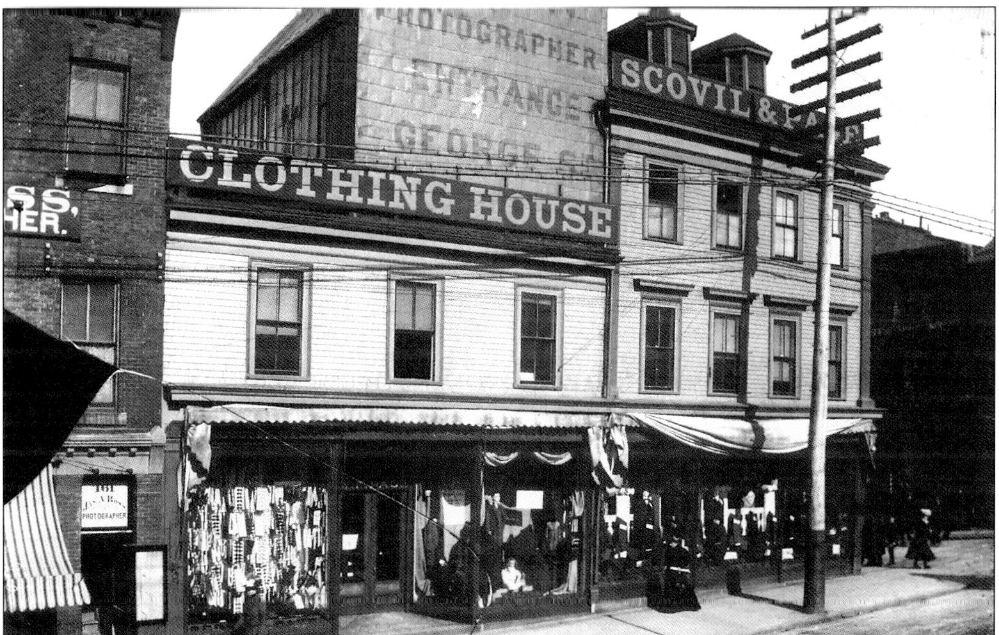

The face of shopping in 1901 was an interesting one. The F.W. Page store on Barrington Street was loaded with clothes to purchase, or products to make one's own. Alongside, Jas. A. Ross, Photographer's Building was located, while some major competition, the Notman Studios, looms large, advertising above Page's Clothing House. As this picture was taken by the Notman Studio, one wonders if the intended subject was the store or the self-publicity. Scovil & Page's General Store forms the end of the block. (Courtesy of the Photograph Collection, Public Archives of Nova Scotia, Notman Collection, #9697.)

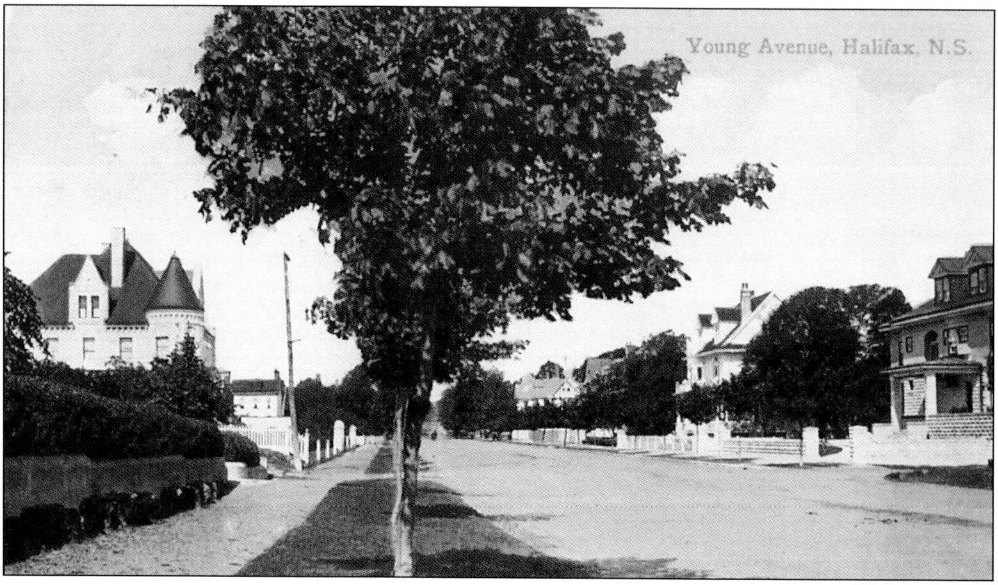

Young Avenue, which extends from South Park Street to Point Pleasant Park, housed some of the largest residential houses in Halifax. Still an exclusive neighbourhood today, little has changed since this early 1900s picture postcard, save for the paving of the road and trees obscuring many of the houses seen here.

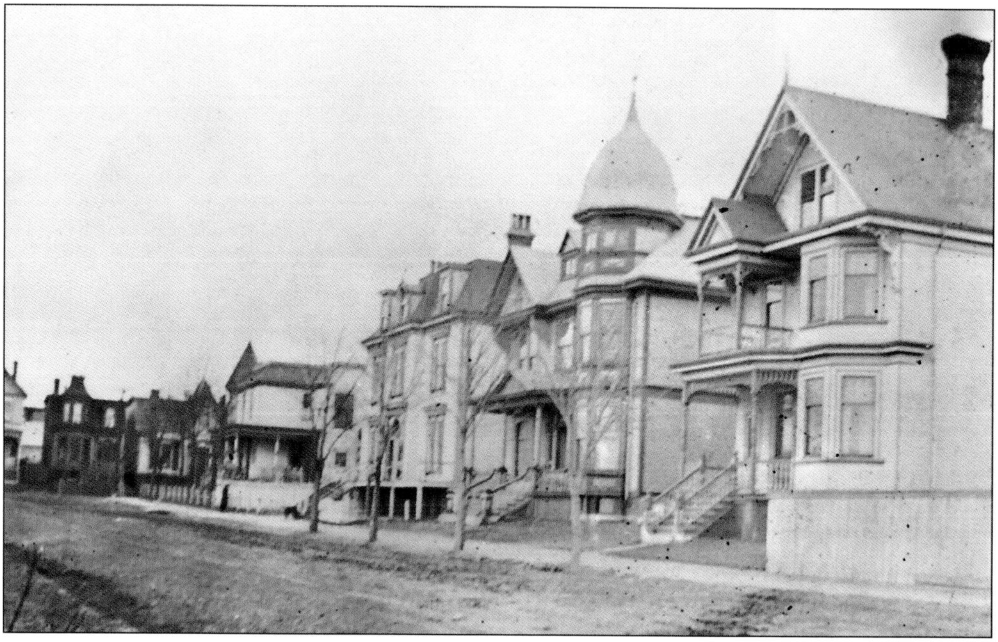

College Street, which only runs from Robie Street through to South Park Street, boasts some fine Edwardian architecture, some of which still exists today. This photograph, taken in the early 1900s, is one of the earliest existing photographs of the street. (Courtesy of the Photograph Collection, Public Archives of Nova Scotia, J.A. Irvine Collection, Album #36, #19.)

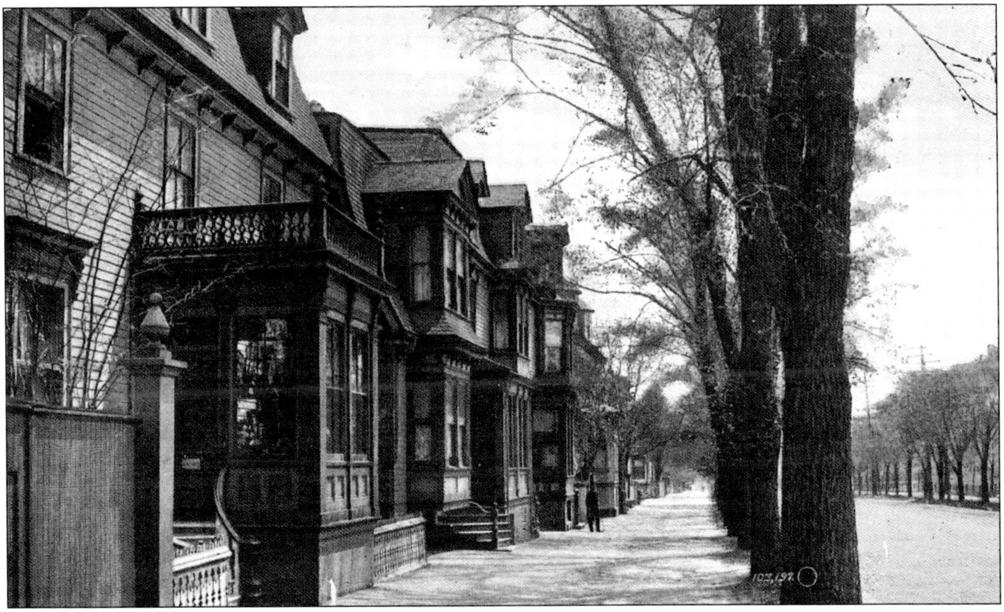

South Park Street, which runs from the Public Gardens at the intersection of Sackville Street across to Inglis Street where it becomes Young Avenue, has a mix of scenery along its length. Along with the splendid housing seen here, it also boasts the Public Gardens, Victoria Park, the Lord Nelson Hotel, and the Victoria General Hospital as its occupants.

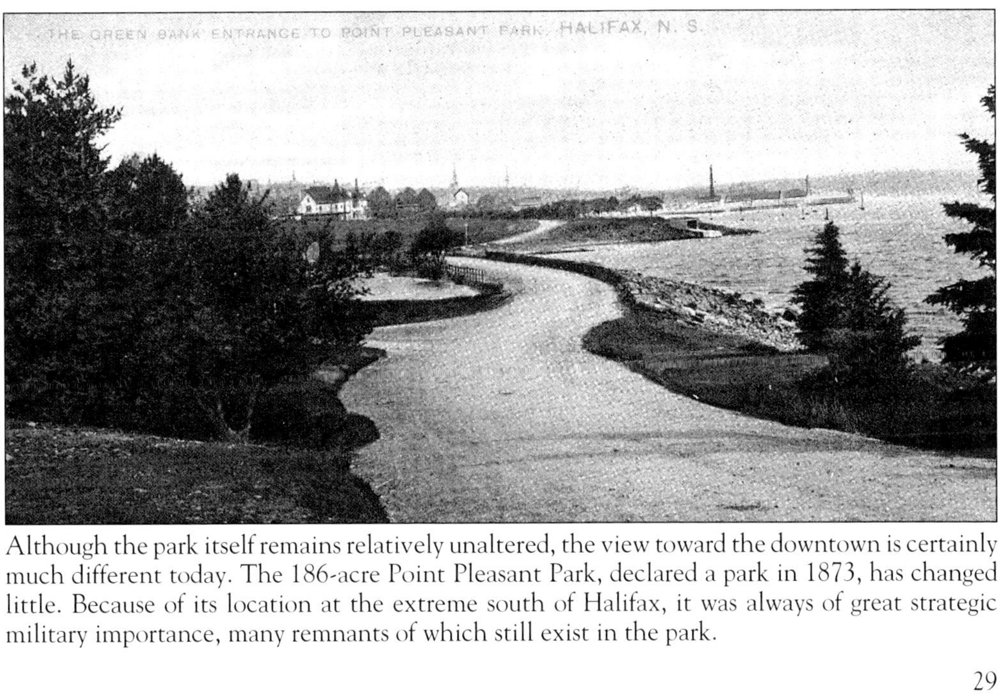

Although the park itself remains relatively unaltered, the view toward the downtown is certainly much different today. The 186-acre Point Pleasant Park, declared a park in 1873, has changed little. Because of its location at the extreme south of Halifax, it was always of great strategic military importance, many remnants of which still exist in the park.

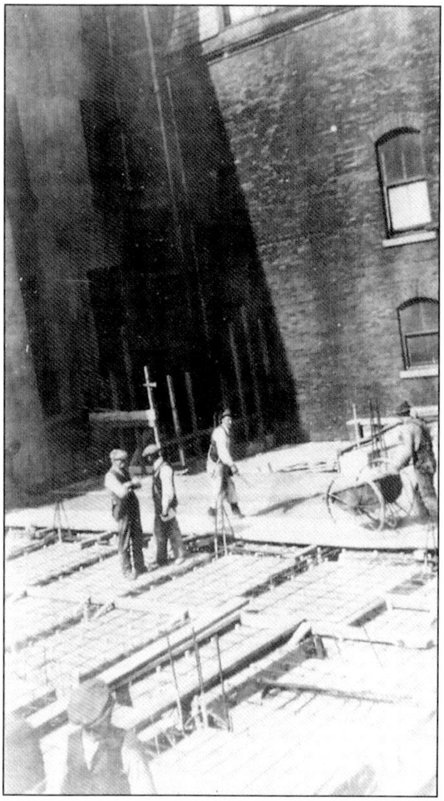

The street scenes have always constantly changed in Halifax for a number of reasons, including fire, explosions, expansion, and dereliction. And so construction is one scene which builds a connection between this section of the book and the next. In the decade commencing 1910, construction of the Strand/Garrick/Neptune Theatre commenced on Sackville Street. This photograph is taken looking towards the back of the Church of England Institute Building on Barrington Street. (Courtesy of the Photograph Collection, Public Archives of Nova Scotia, William H. Noonan fonds, #2.)

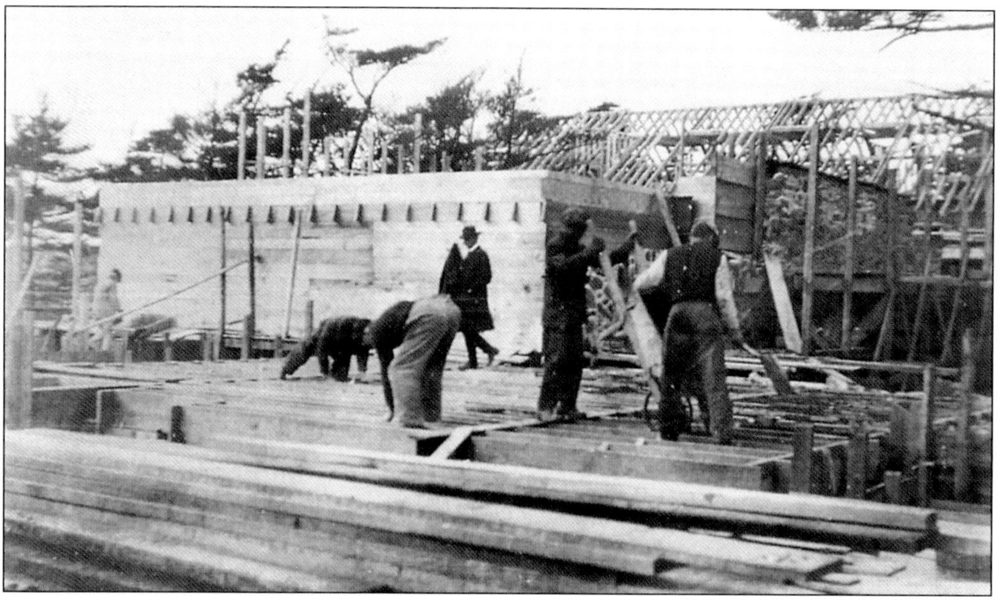

Dalhousie University originally existed at the north end of the Grand Parade, however it grew so rapidly that it moved into the present Forrest Building in the 1880s, a hint of greater expansion to come over the next century. Here is part of the construction of Sheriff Hall at the University's South Street location in 1920. (Courtesy of the Photograph Collection, Public Archives of Nova Scotia, William H. Noonan fonds, #11.)

Three

Government and Commercial Buildings

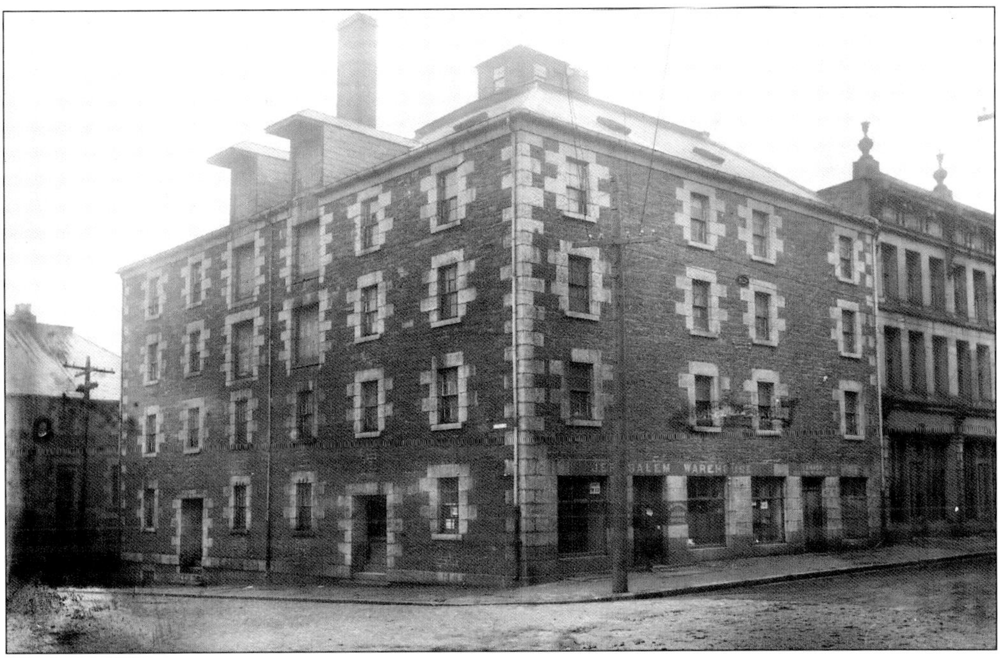

Pictured here is the Jerusalem Warehouse, J.E. Morse Company, built in 1841 on Water Street. (Courtesy of the Photograph Collection, Public Archives of Nova Scotia, 1992-455.)

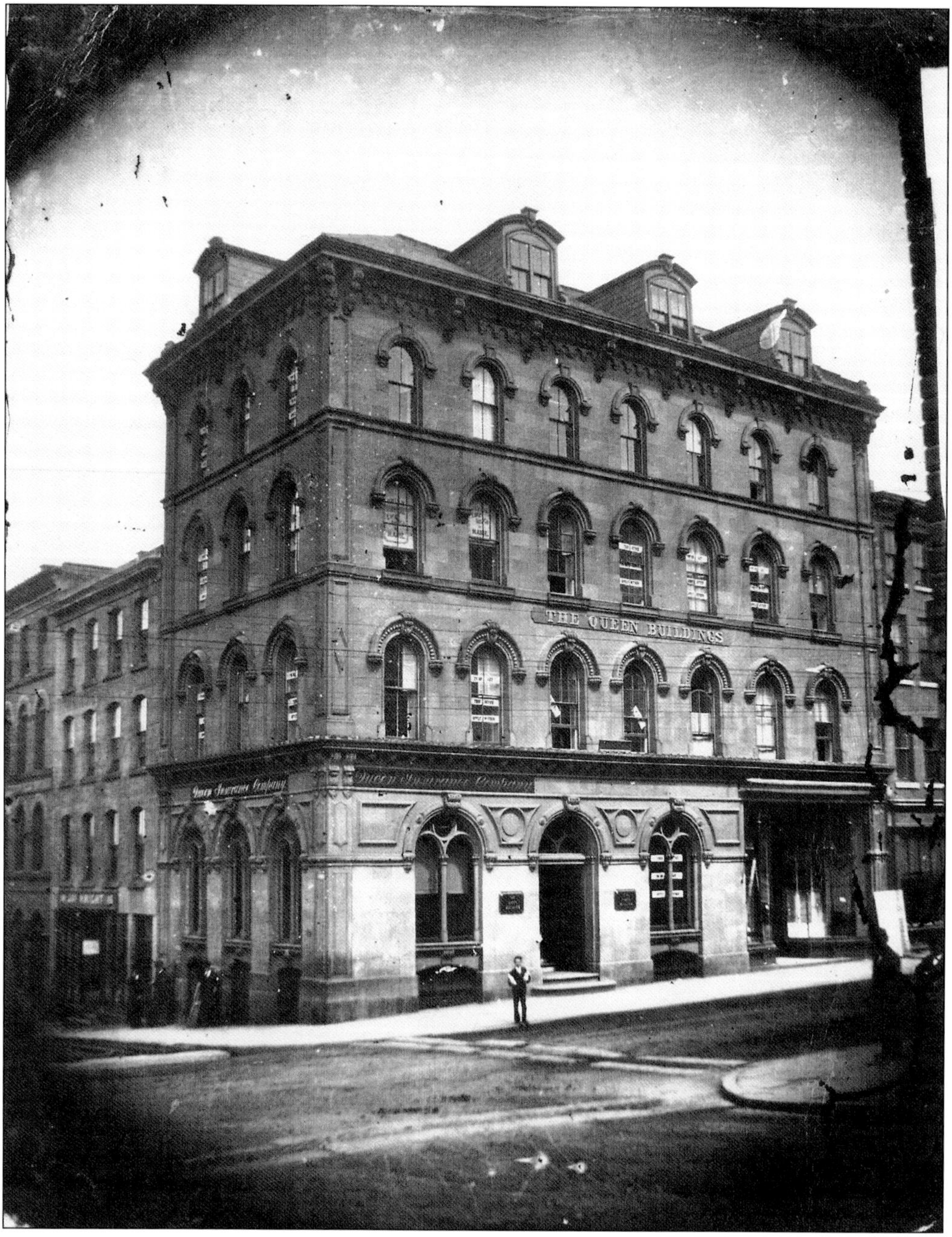

The Queen Buildings at the corner of Hollis and Prince Streets housed a number of different companies. The Queen Insurance Company, as well as other life insurance companies co-existed in the building *c.* 1894, although a surprising number of "To Be Let This Office, Apply Within" signs are clearly visible in the windows. (Courtesy of the Photograph Collection, Public Archives of Nova Scotia, Notman Collection, #4104.)

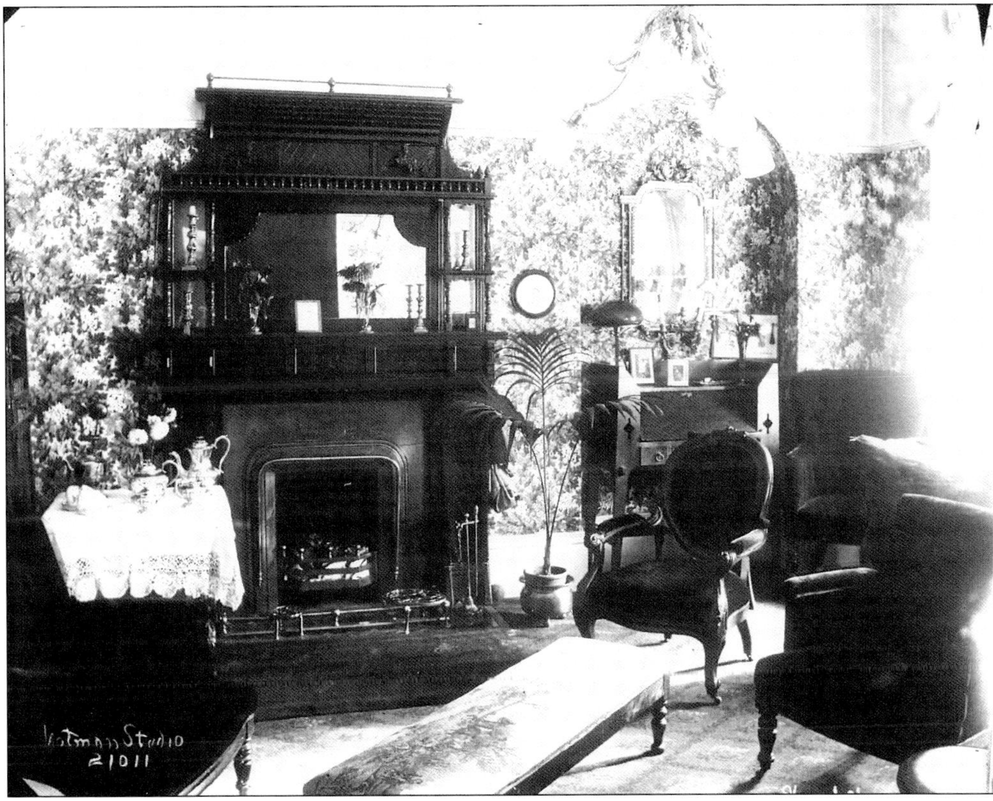

The Queen Hotel on Hollis Street, as noted in the previous section, was one of the most exclusive hotels in the city. This picture of the interior of one of the rooms, the Persian Room, taken c. 1912, shows the exquisite furnishing and elaborate decoration so popular at the time. (Courtesy of the Photograph Collection, Public Archives of Nova Scotia, Notman Collection, #21011.)

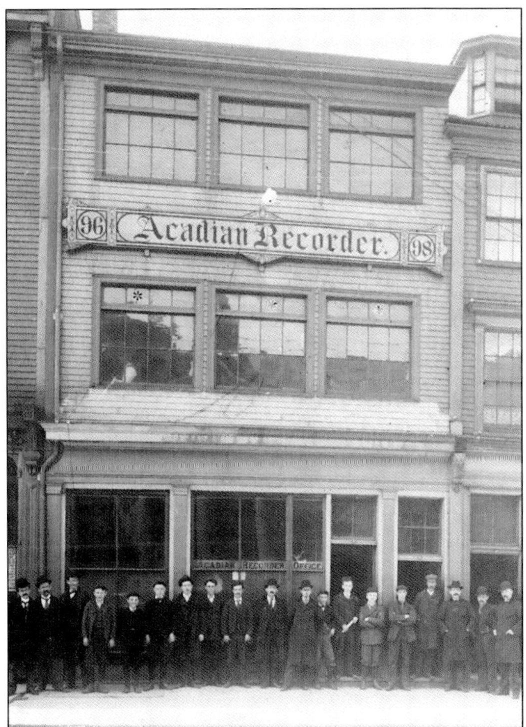

The *Acadian Recorder* was one of five daily newspapers serving a population of less than 100,000 in the 1880s. One of the five, the new *Morning Herald*, started operation in 1875. It survives to this day, but the *Recorder*, which pre-dated it, did not. This photograph was taken outside of their building on Granville Street in the mid-1890s before the Acadian Hotel was built around 1897. (Courtesy of the Photograph Collection, Public Archives of Nova Scotia, Topographical Union Collection c. 1897, #1.)

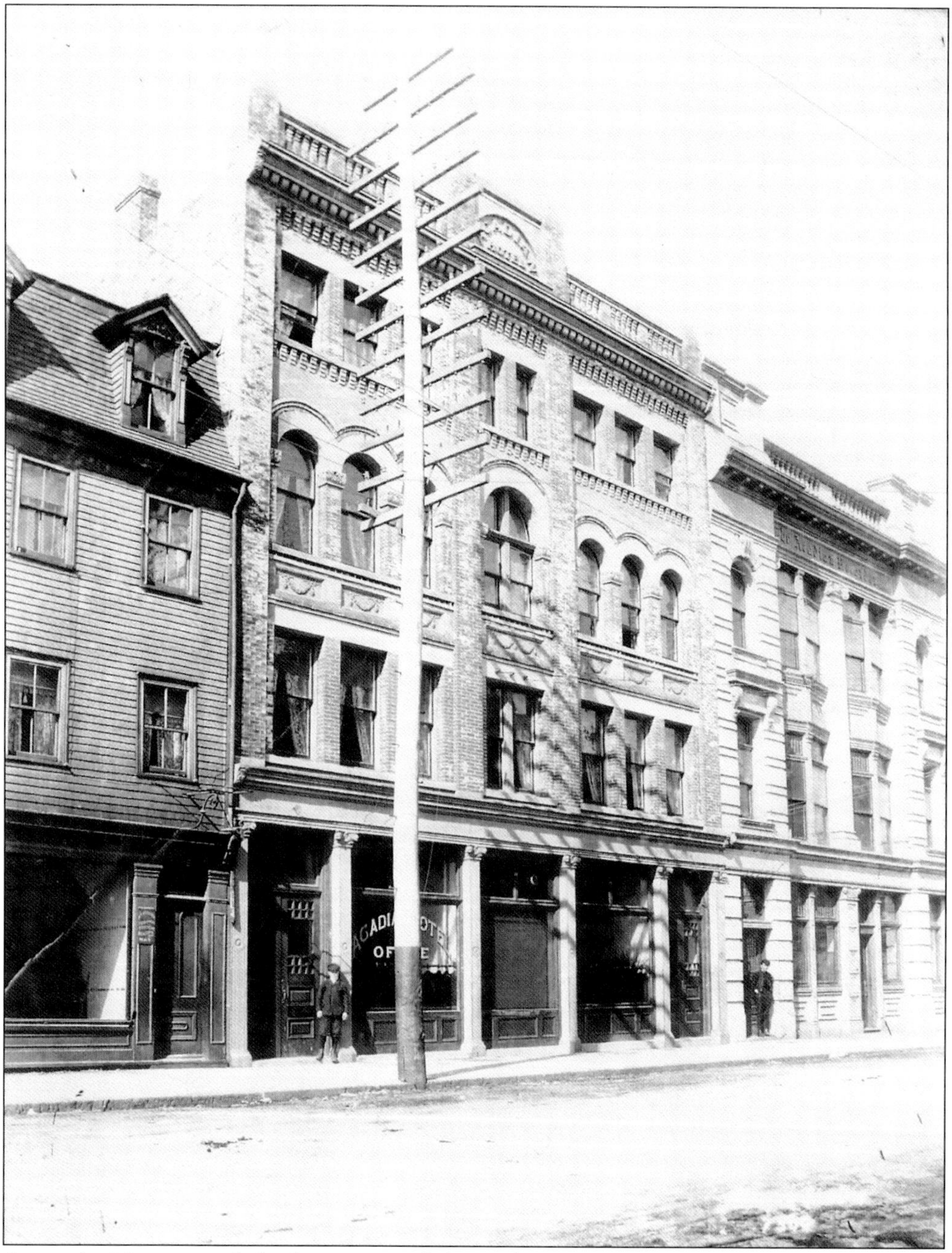

A new building toward the latter part of the 19th century was erected where the *Acadian Recorder* had stood. The new building on Granville Street, shown here *c.* 1900, housed the Acadian Hotel, seen here at centre, and to the left of the picture the Fisher House can be seen. The hotel, like the Queen and Halifax Hotels one street to the east, did not survive. The new *Acadian Recorder* building was on the other side of the new hotel. Halifax's first newspaper was the *Halifax Gazette*, which appeared in 1752, with the first book appearing four years later, the enthralling subject being provincial laws. (Courtesy of the Photograph Collection, Public Archives of Nova Scotia, Notman Collection, #7300.)

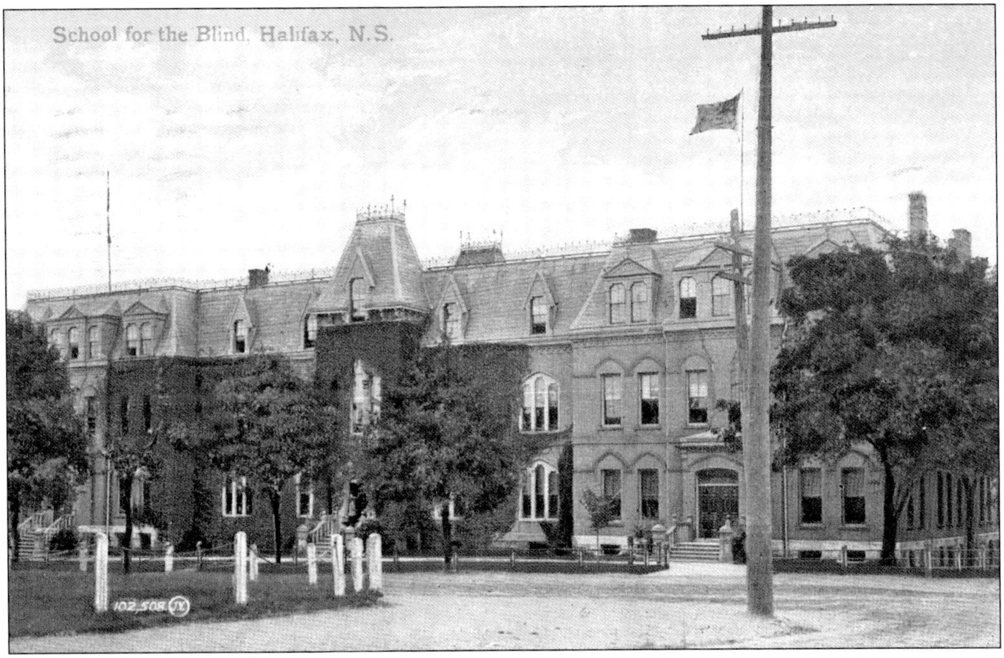

The School for the Blind stood proudly at the intersection of Tower Road and Morris Street, now University Avenue. It is unlikely that modern buildings will usurp the old Victorian building; however, after its demolition, the site became an additional parking lot for the Victorian General Hospital.

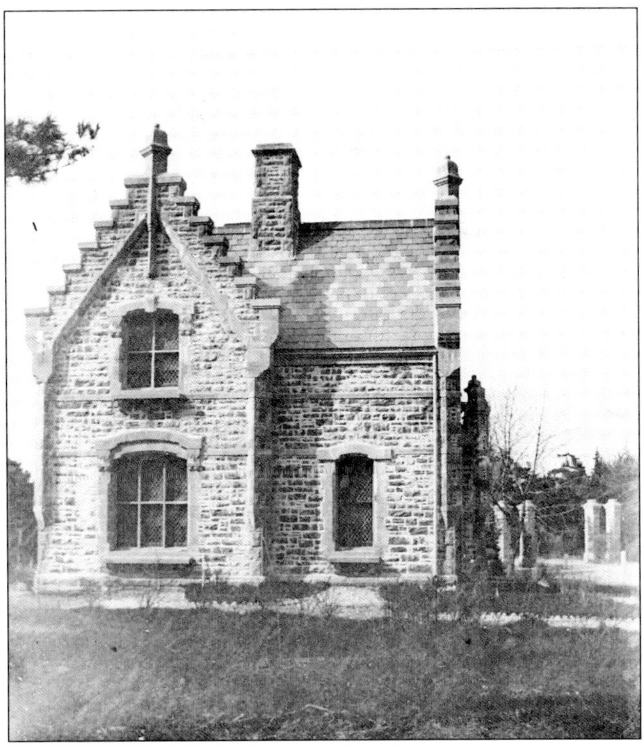

Far south of Halifax lies Point Pleasant Park, which had originally been named Sandwich Point, and was planned by Governor Cornwallis as the original site for the town due to its defensibility. Although it did house Fort Ogilvie, the plans for a town were dropped, and in 1873, it became a park. This turn-of-the-century picture shows the Gatekeepers Lodge which still stands today. (Courtesy of the Photograph Collection, Public Archives of Nova Scotia, J.A. Irvine Collection, Album #37, #47.)

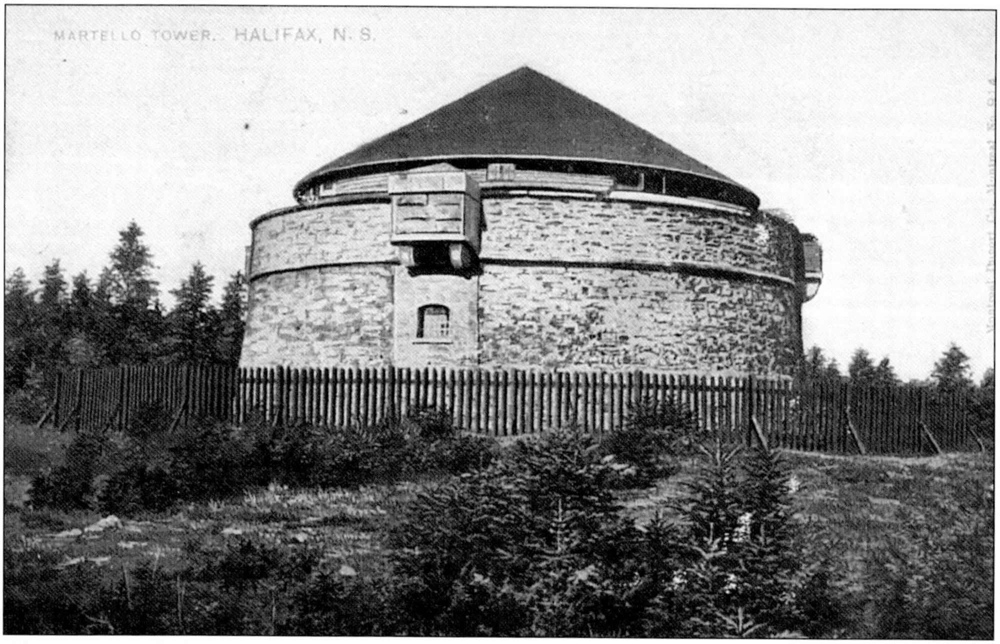

Also contained close to the centre of Point Pleasant Park is the Prince of Wales Tower, built in 1796–97 by Prince Edward, Duke of Kent, the father of Queen Victoria. It was the first of its kind in North America, of what later was called the Martello Tower. The original intent was to protect British sea batteries from potential French attack. Three such towers existed in the area, the others being at York Redoubt and Fort Clarence. Only this one remains today.

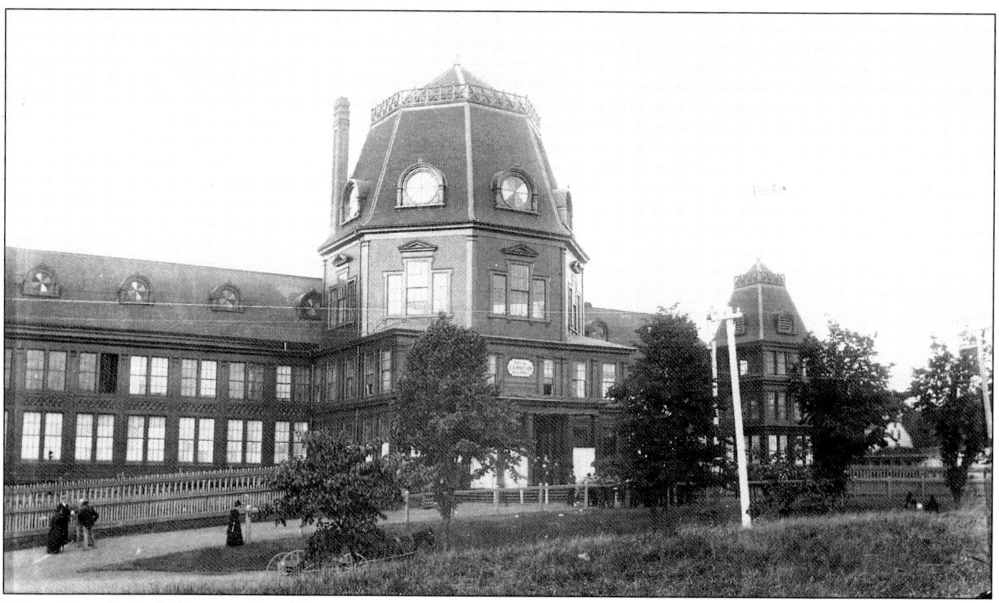

The Royal Exhibition Building, *c.* 1900, on Tower Road, was one of several Exhibition Buildings that sprang up around the city in 1897 and 1898. There were many exhibits in the buildings, from manufacturing to agriculture, as well as balls and other cultural events. One of the Exhibition Buildings on Windsor Street was destroyed by the Halifax Explosion. (Courtesy of the Photograph Collection, Public Archives of Nova Scotia, Notman Collection, #69971.)

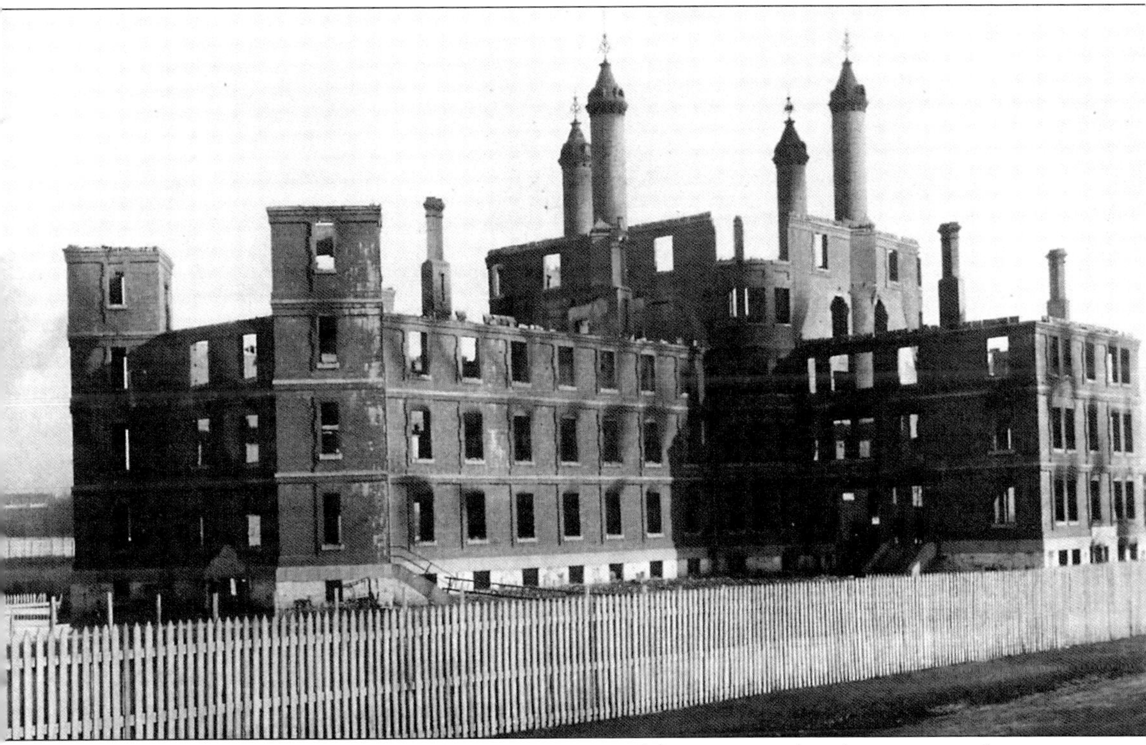

The Poor Asylum, located on South Street, was noted for its unusual architecture, and was at the time the second largest building in Nova Scotia. However a fire started on November 6, 1882, in the basement bake-shop, and due to poor management, no fire prevention measures, and no fire escapes, bed-ridden occupants were trapped on the fifth floor of the building where ladders could not reach. Faces appeared at the windows only to fall into the flames as the floor collapsed. According to the *Acadian Recorder* report on the following day, the "stench of burning flesh was sickening." This picture, taken around two years after the disaster, just prior to the building being blown down by the Royal Engineers on December 16, 1884, served as a chilling reminder and monument to the 31 lives lost on that night. (Courtesy of the Photograph Collection, Public Archives of Nova Scotia, Halifax: Buildings 53.4.)

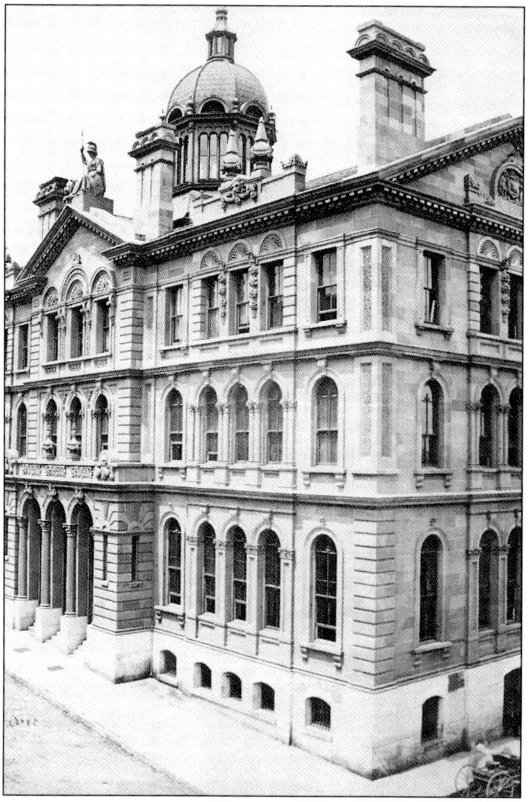

This is a photograph of the magnificent Custom House and post office situated at the corner of Hollis Street and Cheapside, taken *c.* 1870. The architecture made this one of the most outstanding buildings in the Province, and it still stands today, in an altered and renovated form, as the Art Gallery of Nova Scotia. (Courtesy of the Photograph Collection, Public Archives of Nova Scotia, Notman Collection, #39063.)

Government House, which faces Hollis Street, was completed at a great financial cost. It was first occupied in 1807 by then Gov. Sir John Wentworth. His family's stay in the beautiful home lasted only until 1808 when unknown to him he was ousted by a new governor, Sir George Prevost. The building remains the home of the Crown's representative in Nova Scotia, and it is considered to be the oldest continuously utilized official residence in North America. (Courtesy of the Photograph Collection, Public Archives of Nova Scotia.)

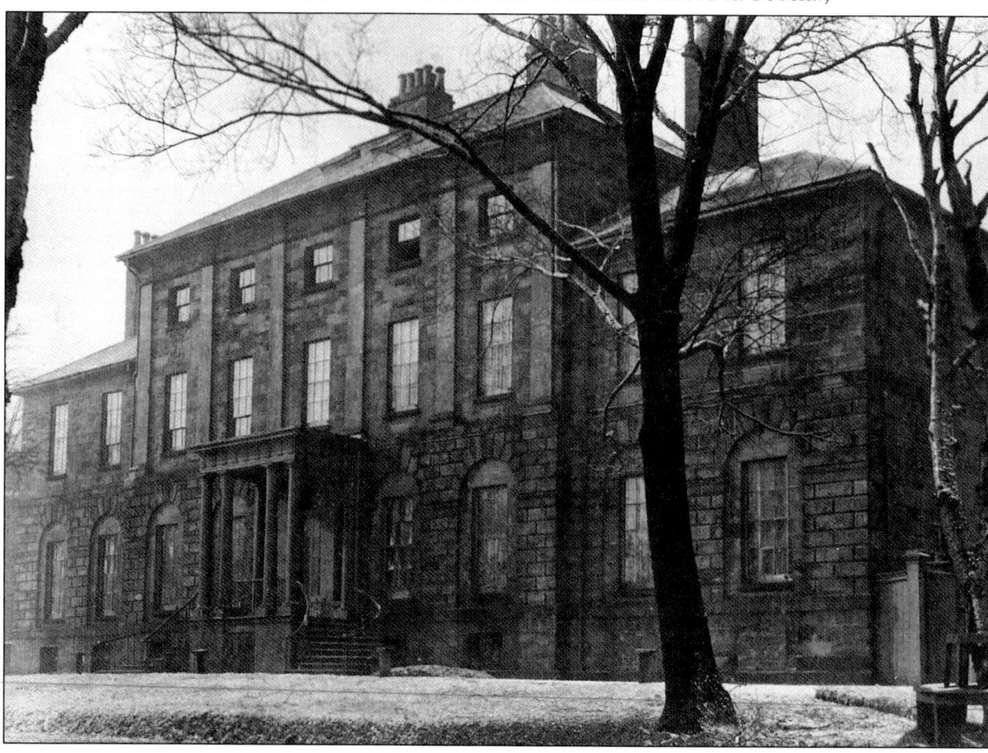

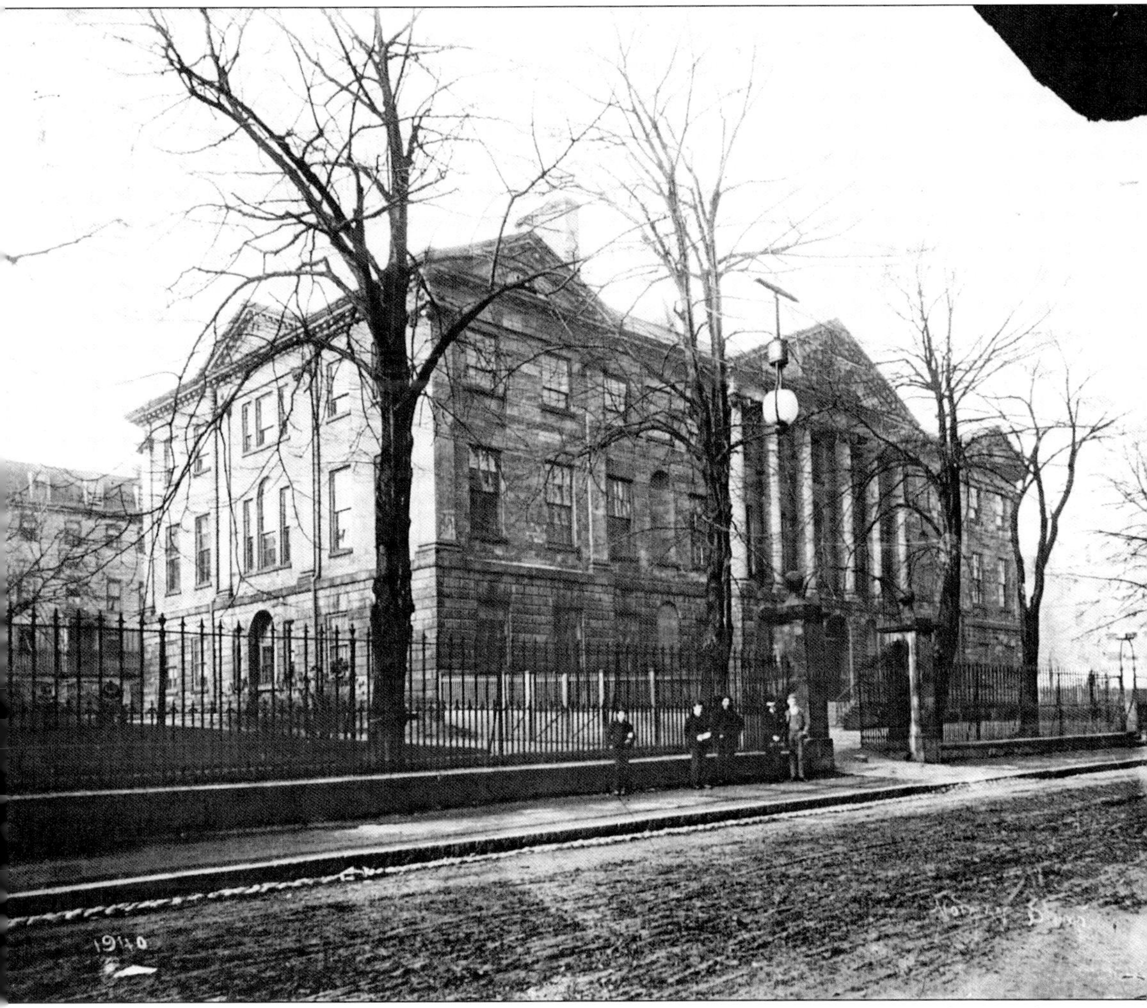

Province House, the seat of the Nova Scotia government, was begun in 1811 and opened in 1819, and is still located at 1726 Hollis Street. It became the home of Britain's first overseas self-government. Charles Dickens, who visited the city, deemed it, "a gem of Georgian architecture." The two lamp standards which stand outside the Hollis Street entrance were taken from the famous Waterloo Bridge which spans the Thames in London. When it opened, the cost for this beautiful building was £52,000. (Courtesy of the Photograph Collection, Public Archives of Nova Scotia, Notman Collection, #1940.)

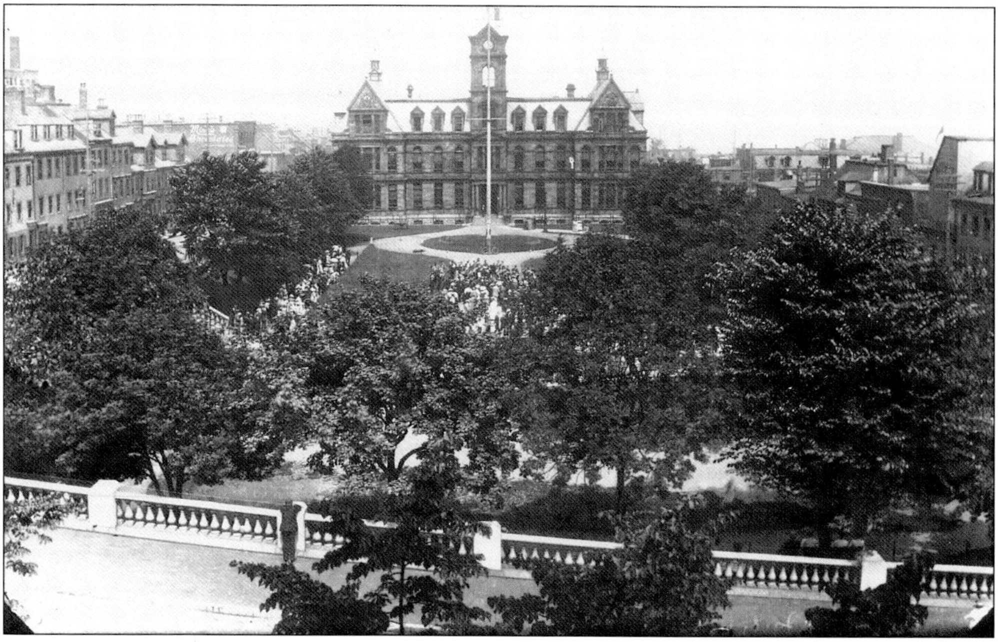

Above is an unidentified parade taking place in the Grand Parade in July of 1907. At the far end of the Grand Parade stands the new city hall. In 1841, after incorporation, a red brick building was used as the city hall, but by 1885 it was becoming unsuitable. The new city hall had one entrance at the north end of the Grand Parade and another on Duke Street for the police station, jail cells, and courtroom. (Courtesy of the Photograph Collection, Public Archives of Nova Scotia, Notman Collection, #15497.)

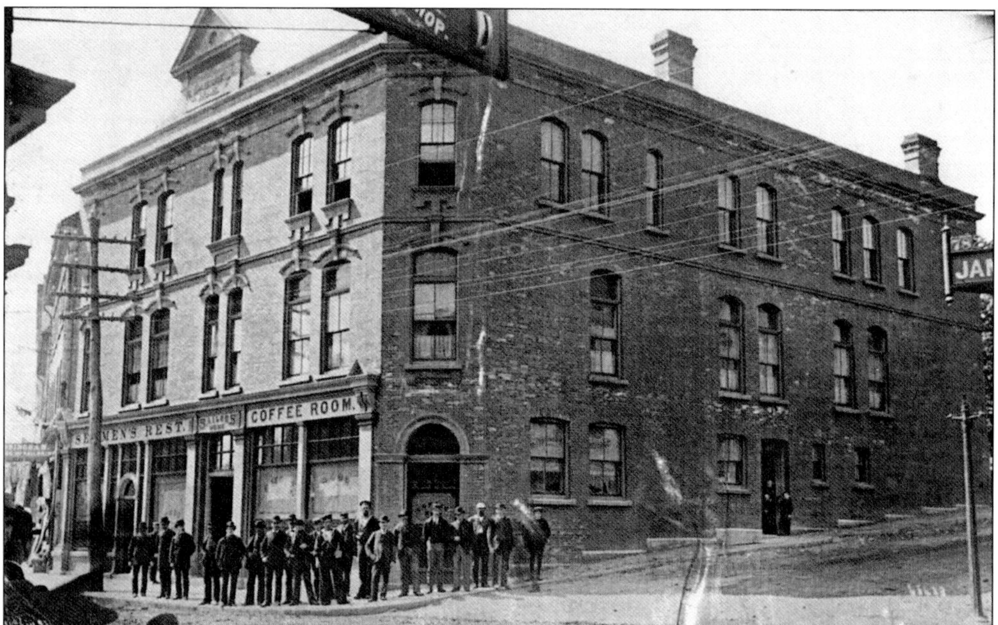

An extremely popular building, the Sailor's Home and Seamen's Restaurant and Coffee Room was located at 16–18 Upper Water Street. This photograph is from c. 1885. (Courtesy of the Photograph Collection, Public Archives of Nova Scotia, Notman Collection, #65423.)

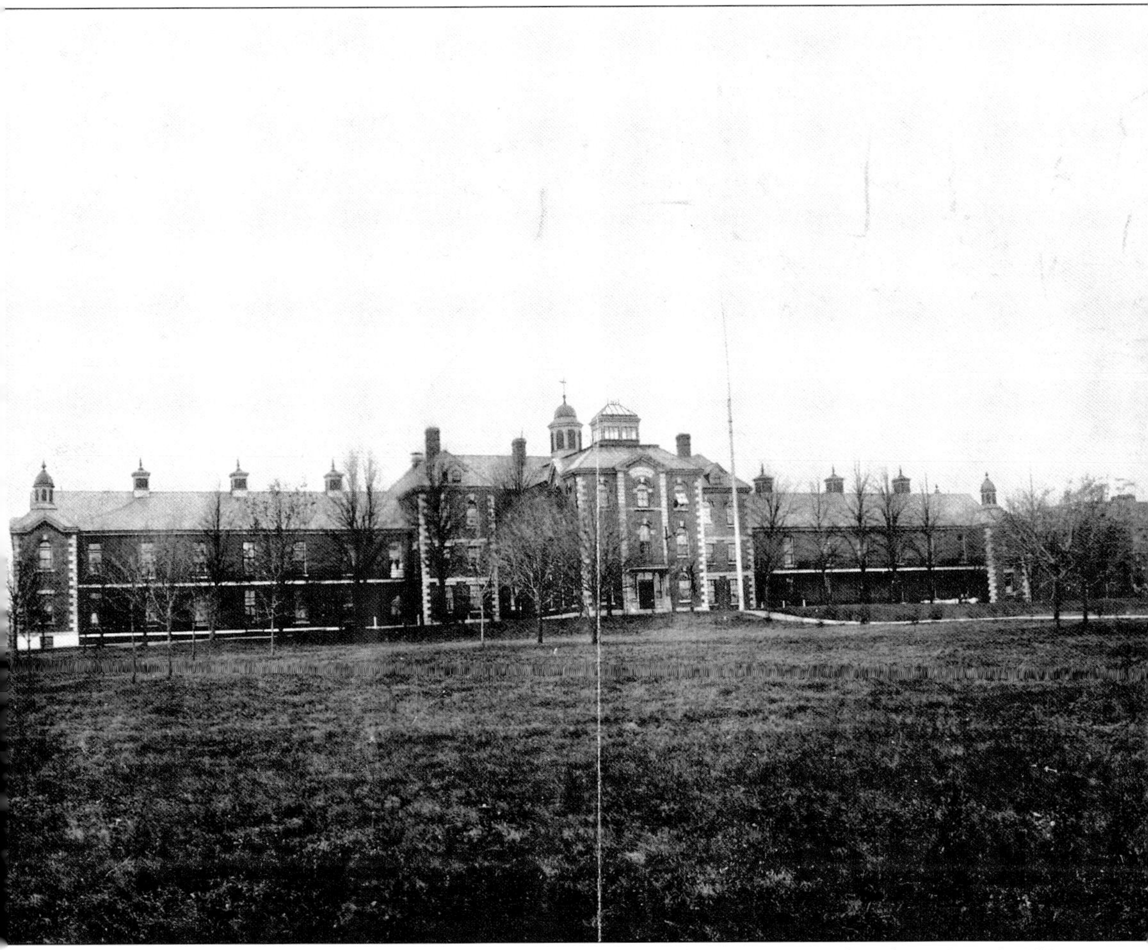

In 1857, a Mr. Gordon drew up plans for a new city hospital that was completed in May of 1859, at a cost of $38,000. Maintained by the city alone until May 1, 1867, it was then transferred by an Act of Provincial Legislation to the Commissioners of the Poor Asylum. In 1886, the Provincial and City Hospital, as it was known in this c. 1875 picture, was renamed the Victoria General Hospital and repaired and enlarged at a cost of $20,000. The old building was replaced in 1948. (Courtesy of the Photograph Collection, Public Archives of Nova Scotia, Halifax: Buildings, 53.4.)

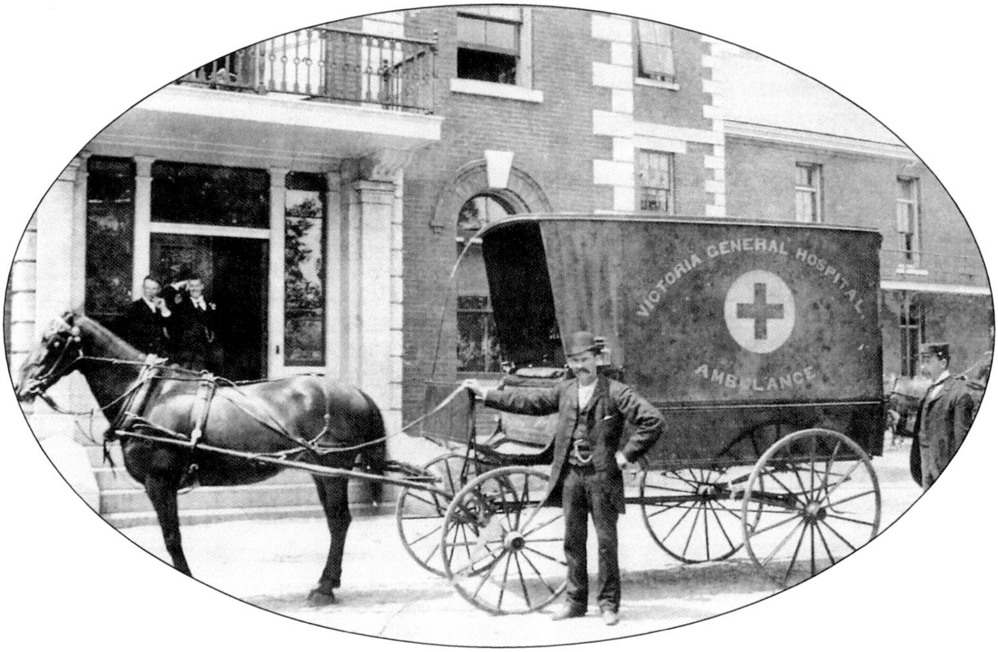

Around 1910, traveling in comfort was a relative thing, especially when it came to being transported in an ambulance. Although galloping around the city was far easier than under current heavy traffic conditions, the speeds at which the ambulances could travel were obviously limited. (Courtesy of the Photograph Collection, Public Archives of Nova Scotia, Notman Collection, #1984.)

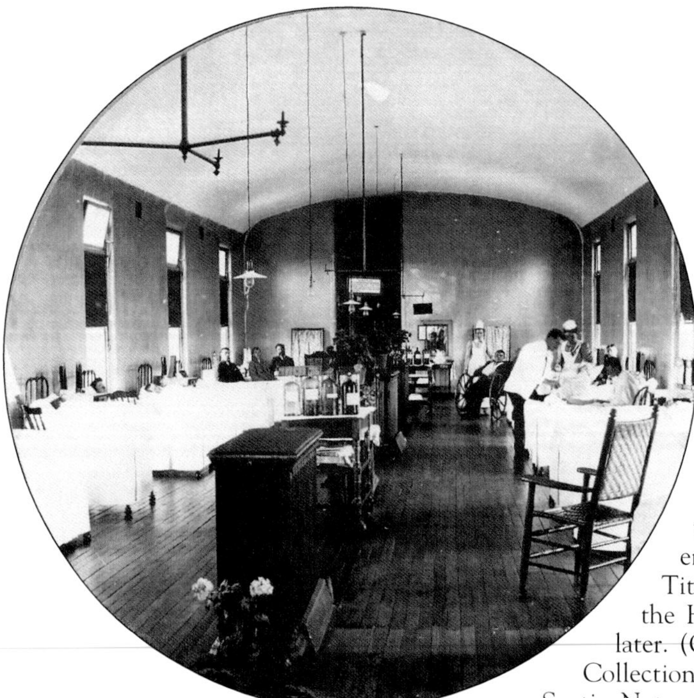

This picture taken inside Ward 42 of the Victoria General Hospital also dates to 1910. Over its 89-year history, the hospital saw many emergencies, including the Titanic disaster of 1912 and the Halifax Explosion five years later. (Courtesy of the Photograph Collection, Public Archives of Nova Scotia, Notman Collection, #2027.)

Four

Monuments and Religious, Educational, and Residential Buildings

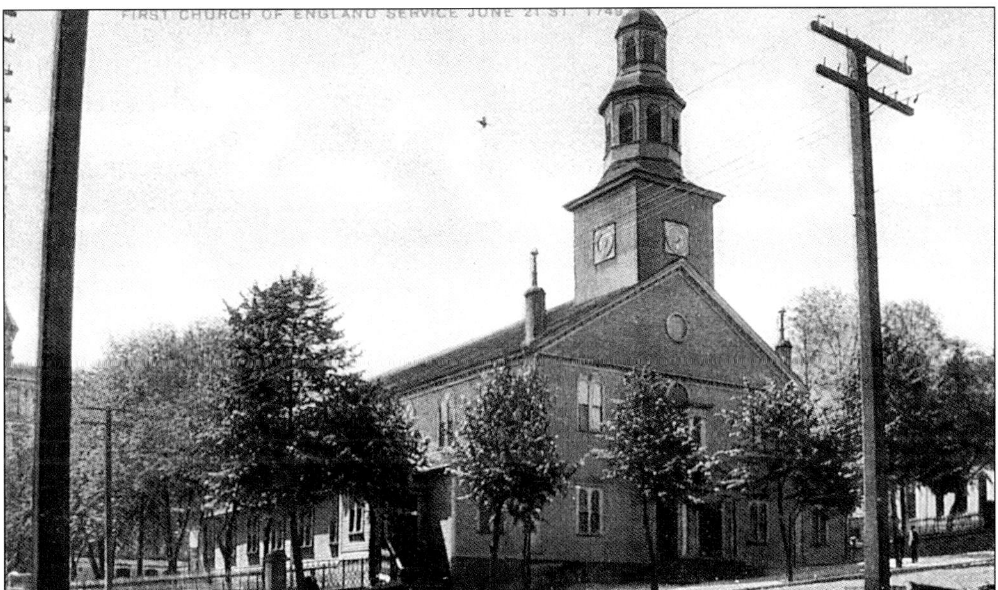

Here is St. Paul's Church, located on Barrington Street, Halifax.

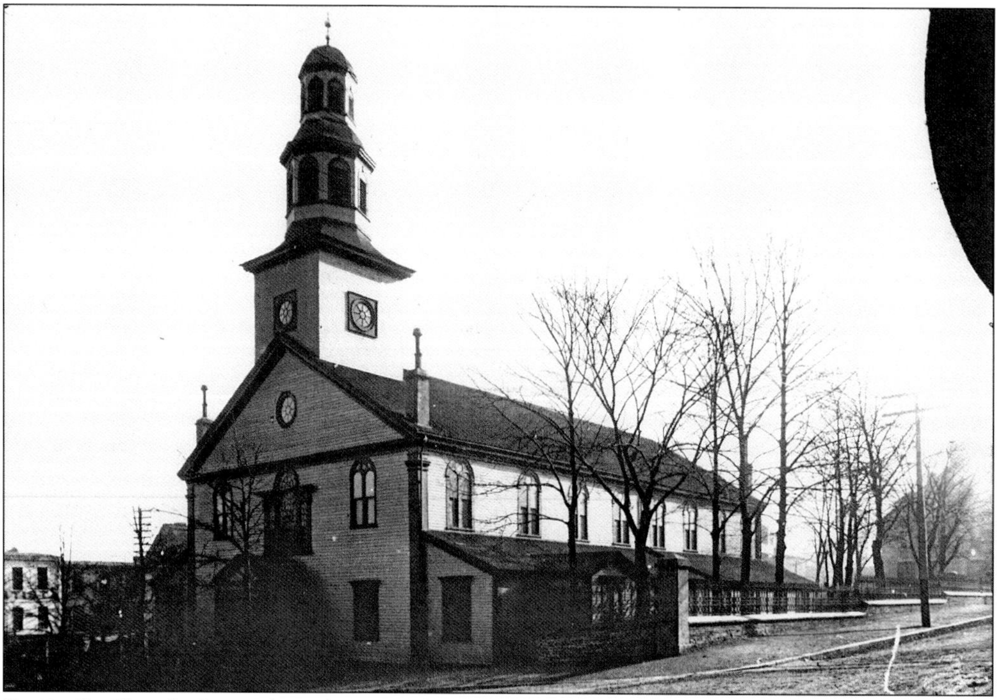

St. Paul's Church, located on the Grand Parade, was made in 1749 in New England and then assembled on site. It opened in September of 1750, remains the oldest Protestant church in Canada, and was Britain's first overseas Cathedral. It is often deemed the "Westminster Abbey of the New World." A piece of wood from the *Mont Blanc*, one of the ships involved in the Halifax Explosion, is embedded in the church. (Courtesy of the Photograph Collection, Public Archives of Nova Scotia, Notman Collection, #53.)

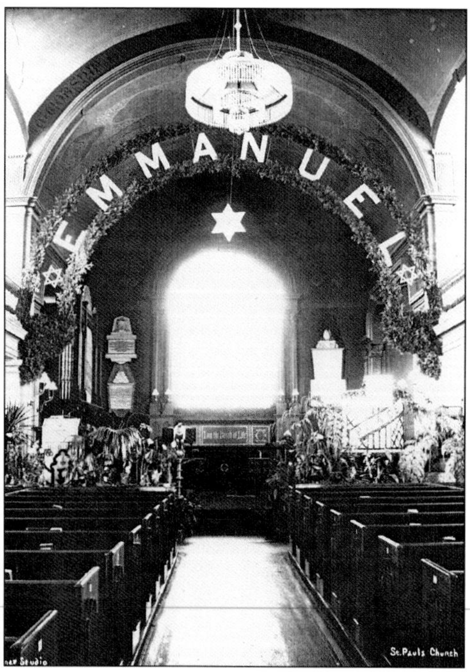

The chancel of St. Paul's Church decorated for Christmas in 1898. The newspapers of the day paid little attention, and amid the usual bad news was a single page dedicated to the meaning of Christmas. Few advertisements were to be found, however in the *Halifax Herald* of Christmas Eve 1898, Geo. T. Smith's store on George Street was selling Christmas embroidered lace handkerchiefs, and elsewhere, an advertisement showing a merry Santa stated, "The Secret's Out! Santa Claus drinks Bovril and never Grows Older." (Courtesy of the Photograph Collection, Public Archives of Nova Scotia, Notman Collection, #5993.)

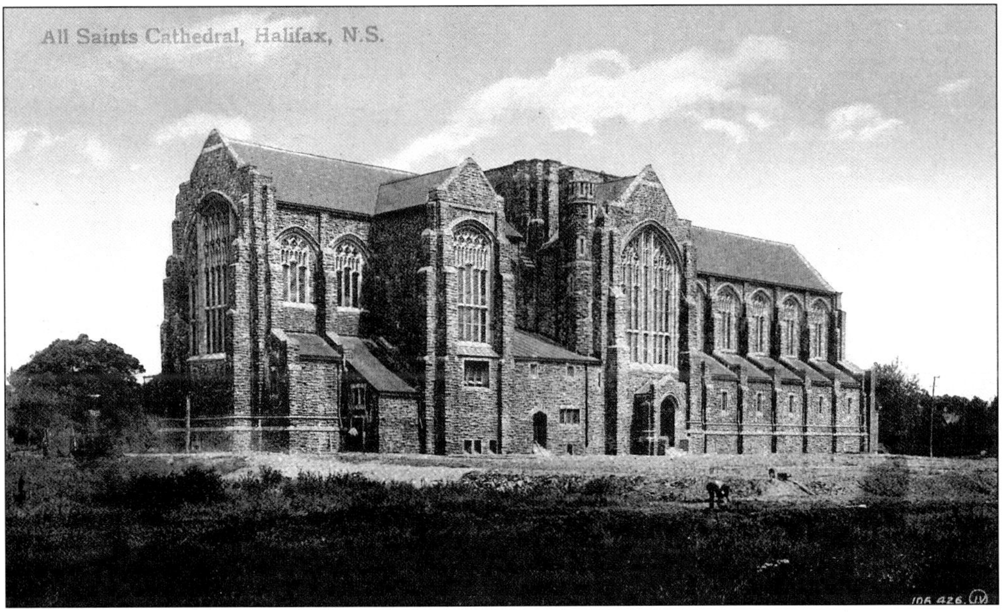

All Saint's Cathedral, seen here in its finishing stages, was opened on September 3, 1910 on the Tower Road site vacated in 1906 after the $18,000 purchase of six lots of the old Exhibition Grounds on Tower Road and Morris Street. The granite for the cathedral was taken from the penitentiary in Point Pleasant Park.

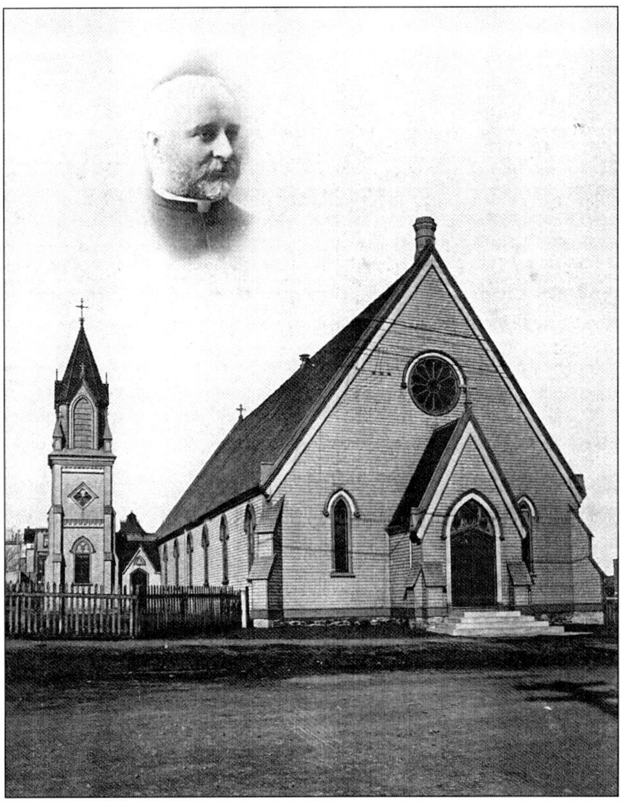

Seen here is St. Stephen's Chapel of Ease, c. 1900, at the corner of Robie Street and Coburg Road, with an inset of Rev. Kenneth Cameron Hind. (Courtesy of the Photograph Collection, Public Archives of Nova Scotia, anonymous oversize collection, #39.)

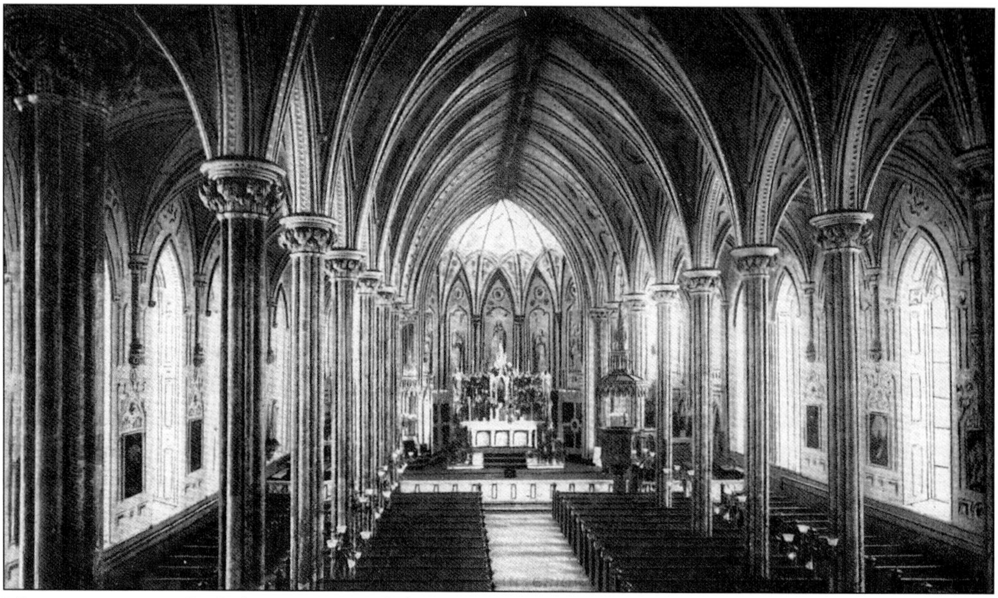

This is a postcard of the interior of the imposing St. Mary's Cathedral. St. Mary's replaced the old church of St. Peter, located opposite Salter Street, a small wooden building painted red. It was the first Roman Catholic place of worship in Halifax and had been built in 1784. When it was replaced, St. Peter's was taken across to Dartmouth to become St. Peter's in that community.

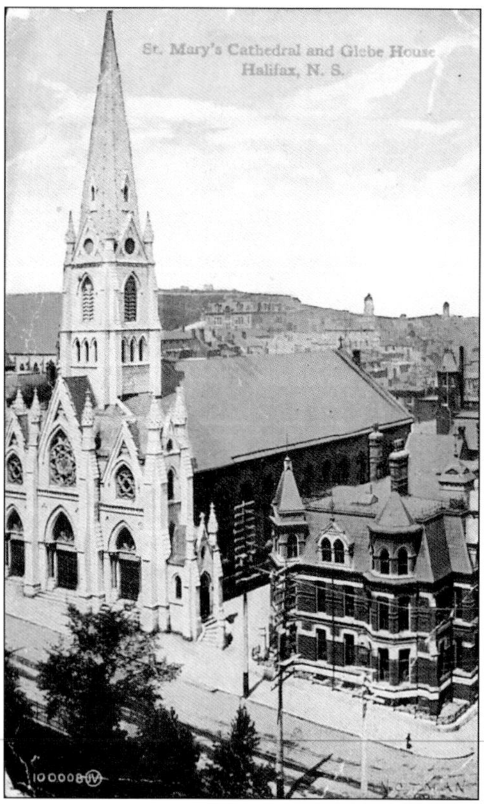

This picture, taken from St. Matthew's spire, shows the domination of the skyline by the 128-foot-high granite steeple of this church situated on Spring Garden Road. The steeple is the tallest polished granite steeple in North America. The cornerstone of the church was laid by Bishop Burke in 1820, but the church was not completed for several years.

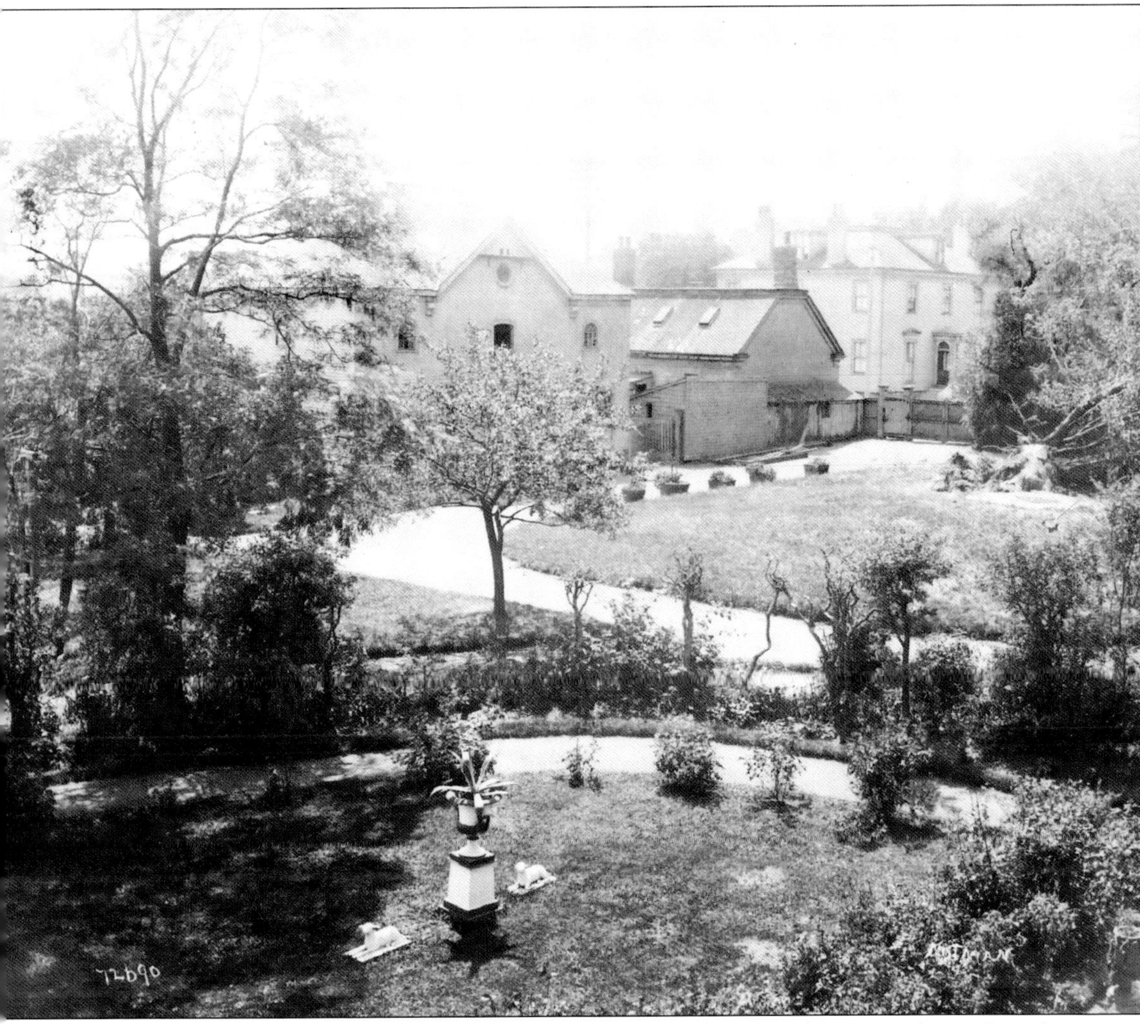

Tobin House, the home of the Hons. James and Michael Tobin, merchants, was located on the south side of South Street between Hollis and Pleasant Streets. Built *c.* 1830, it was demolished on September 28, 1928. Michael Tobin along with Samuel Cunard administered a soup kitchen, which assisted five hundred people a day, and was made necessary by a depression following the end of the War of 1812. James Tobin was one of the shareholders of the first official bank in Halifax, the Halifax Banking Company, which opened in 1825. (Courtesy of the Photograph Collection, Public Archives of Nova Scotia, Notman Collection, #72690.)

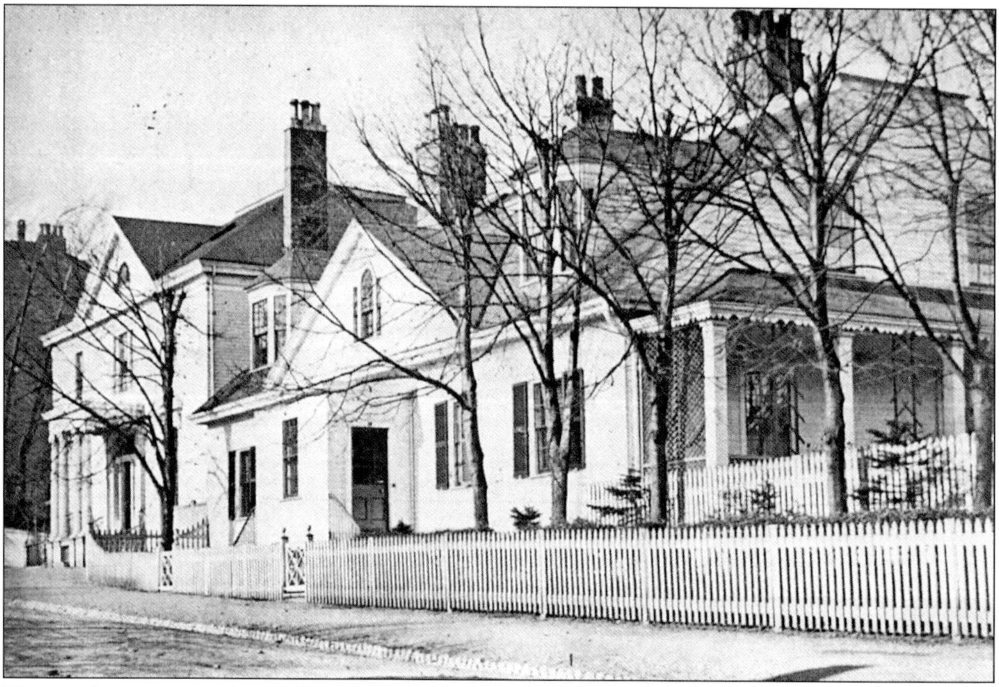

This is The Hive, residence of W.J. Stairs, *c*. 1871. The house adjoining is Hillside, the residence of the Hon. Sir William Young. (Courtesy of the Photograph Collection, Public Archives of Nova Scotia, Stairs Series F:MG1 vol. 3278, folder 13, #5.)

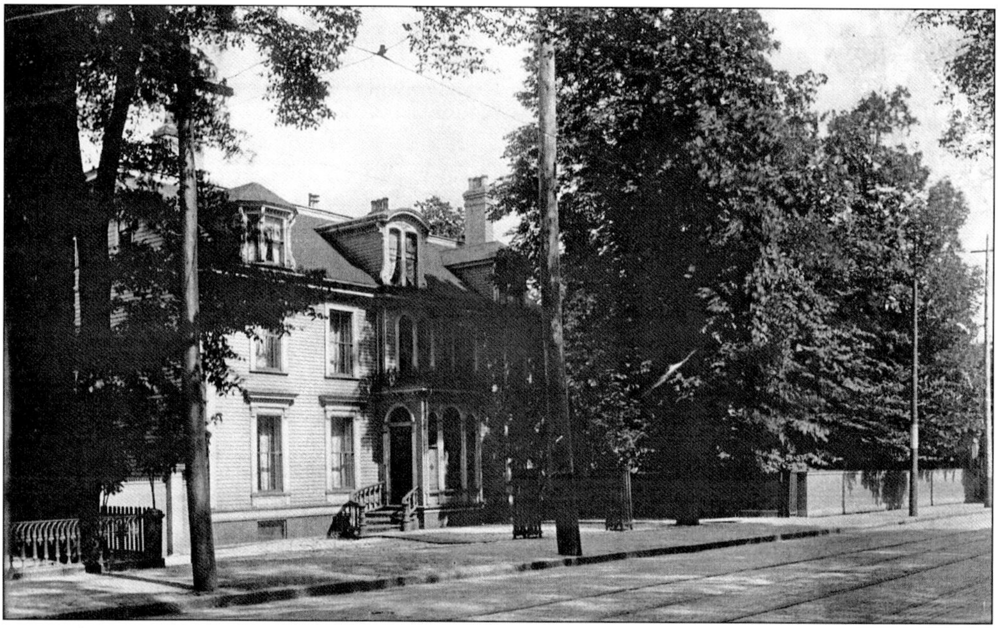

Located at the corner of Barrington and Harvey Streets, this residence had been home to Lawrence Doyle, Sir Edward Henry, and Wiley Smith. This beautiful home, pictured in the 1880s, was demolished to make way for the construction of the Y.W.C.A. building in 1931. (Courtesy of the Photograph Collection, Public Archives of Nova Scotia, Notman Collection #19079.)

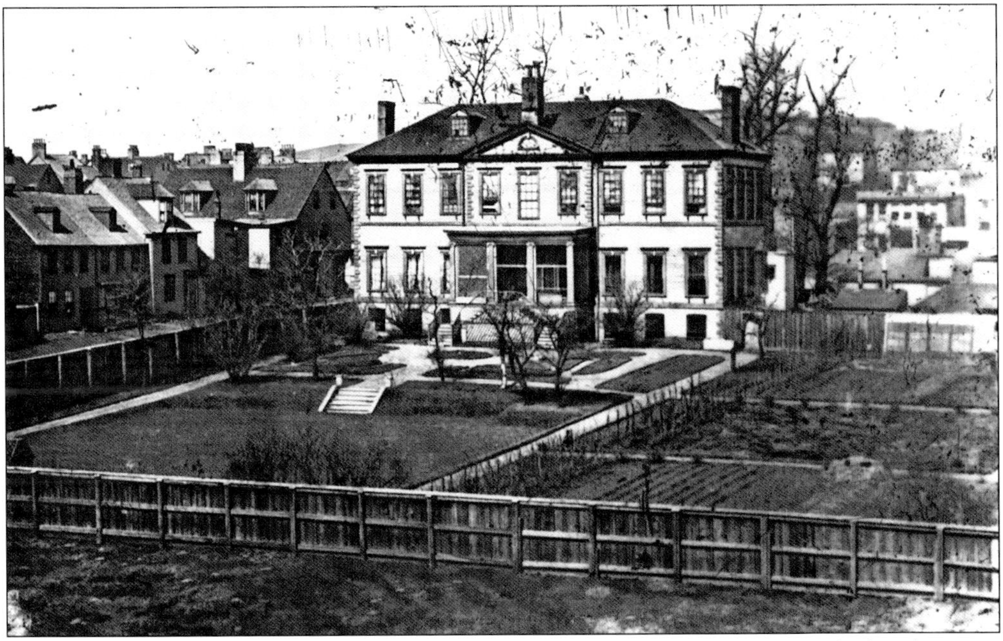

Bellevue, located at the corner of Spring Garden Road and Queen Street, was the headquarters of the General Officer commanding at Halifax. The lot was purchased on April 28, 1800 by the Duke of Kent for $800 from Capt. Robert Dupont of Windsor, NS, specifically for the residence of the Commander-in-Chief. A fire in 1885 led to it being rebuilt in 1886 to 1887. However, it was demolished in 1955. (Courtesy of the Photograph Collection, Public Archives of Nova Scotia.)

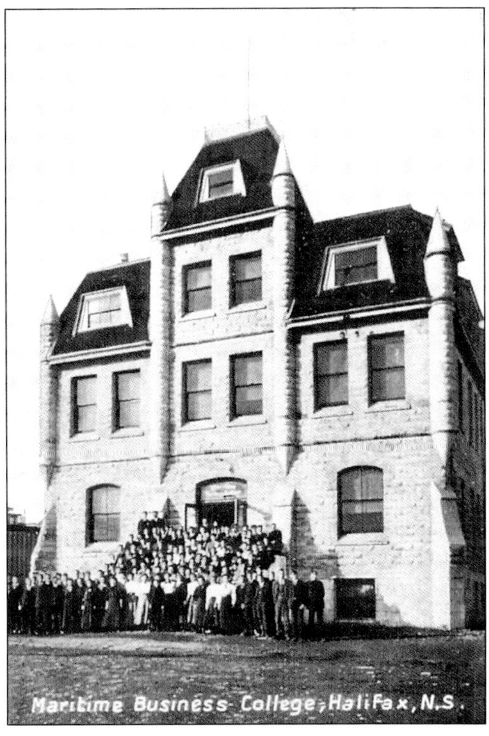

This early 1900s postcard shows the assembled student body and staff of the Maritime Business College. It was sold to Shriners due to courses at the Halifax County Vocational School offering similar programs.

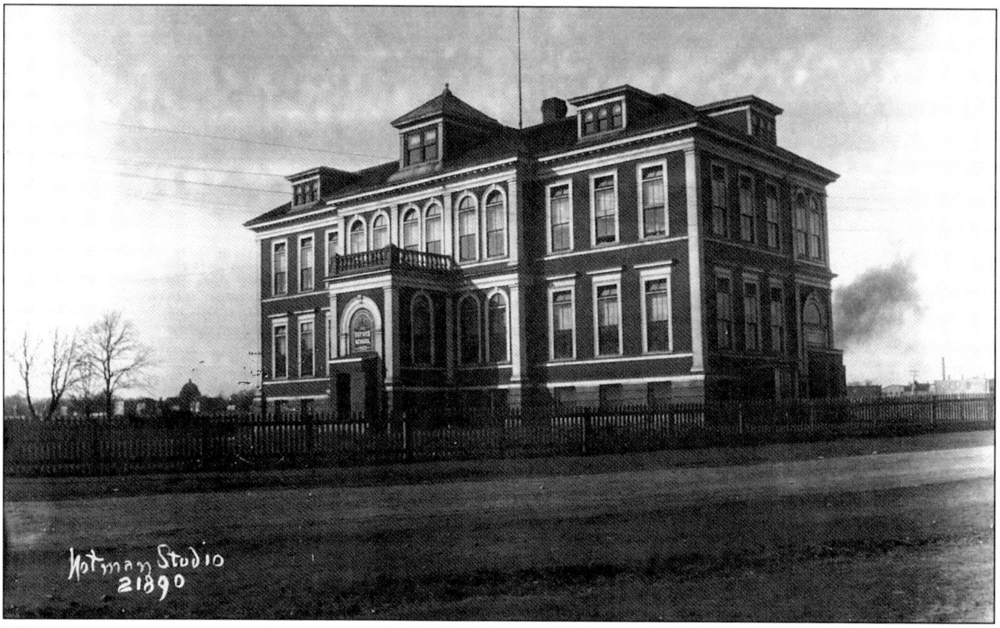

There were many schools scattered throughout Halifax in the early 1900s. This *c.* 1910 photograph shows one of the schools on the outside of the town, the Oxford Public School on Oxford Street, which runs across the city almost connecting the Bedford Basin to the Northwest Arm, a body of water formerly called Sandwich River. The school was demolished in September 1967. (Courtesy of the Photograph Collection, Public Archives of Nova Scotia, Notman Collection, #21890.)

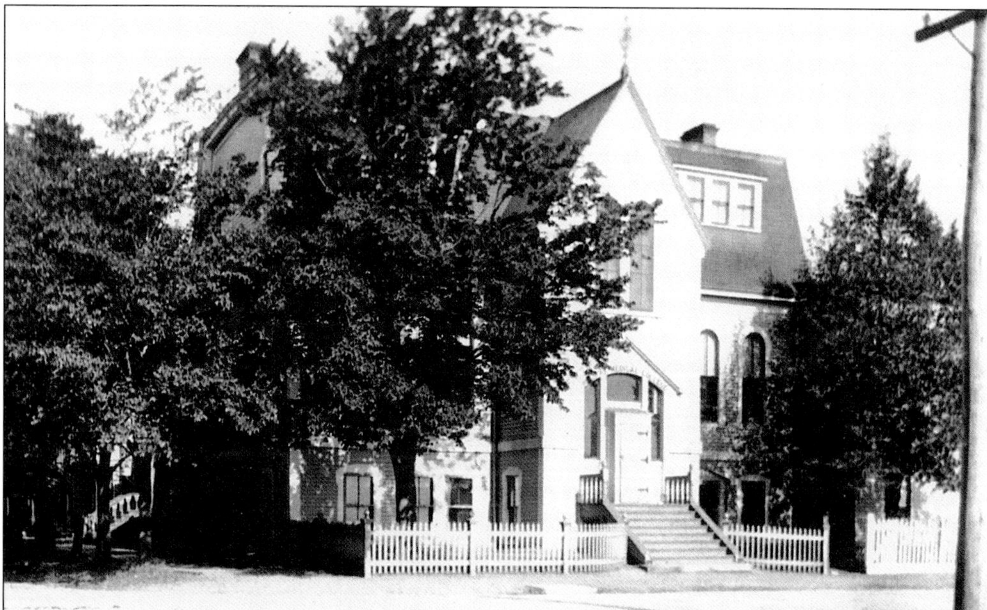

Close to the Dalhousie College Building, this early 1900s image shows the Halifax Medical College, which was located at the corner of College Street and Carlton Street. (Courtesy of the Photograph Collection, Public Archives of Nova Scotia, J.A. Irvine Collection, Album #35, #31.)

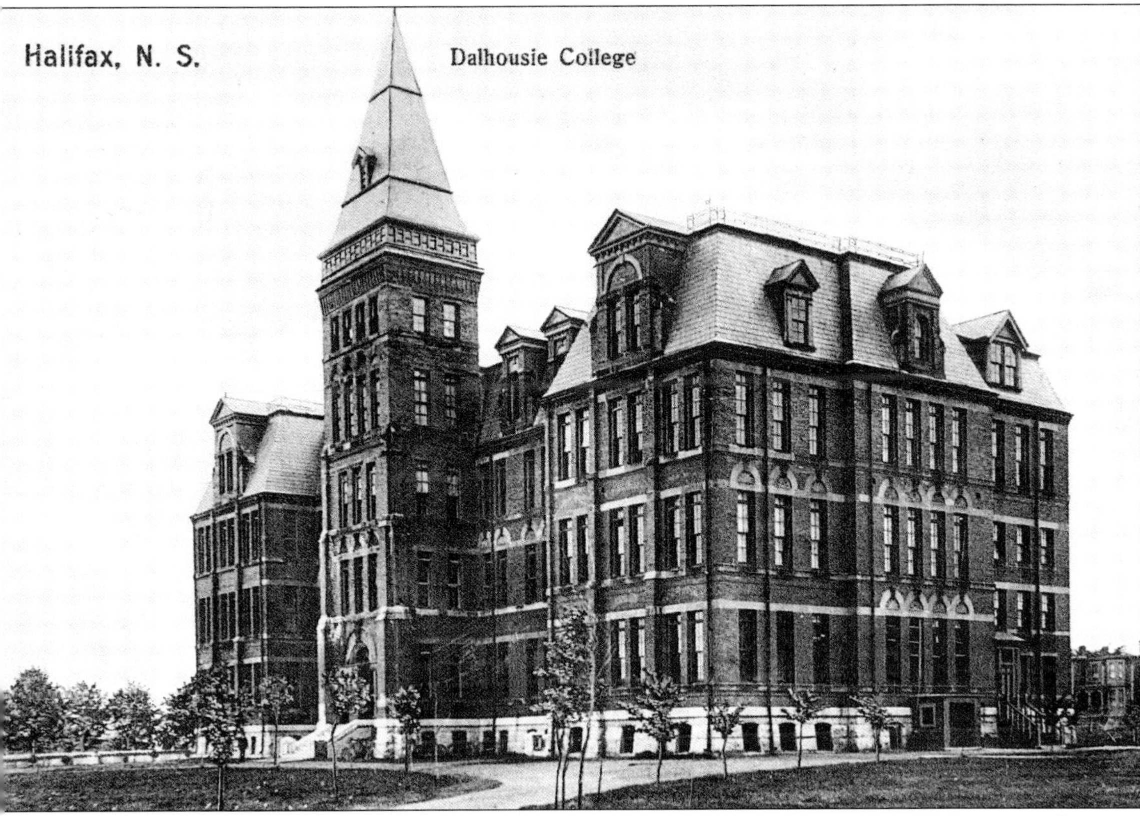

There are currently three universities in Halifax—St. Mary's, Mount Saint Vincent, and Dalhousie University. Technically there is a fourth, the University of King's College, which is the oldest university in Canada dating back to the 18th century. It now is surrounded by Dalhousie University. The original Dalhousie College building was housed on the Grand Parade, the cornerstone of which was laid in 1820 by the lieutenant governor, the Earl of Dalhousie, a Scottish nobleman distinguished during the Spanish Campaign under Lord Wellington. The school was deemed open to all classes and denominations. Once the university had overcome political and religious difficulties, the school grew, until in the 1880s it became clear that if the university was to expand, it needed more space. It then moved over to the Forrest Building on what is now University Avenue. In 1912, the campus expanded by including the Studley estate which had been owned by Judge Croke.

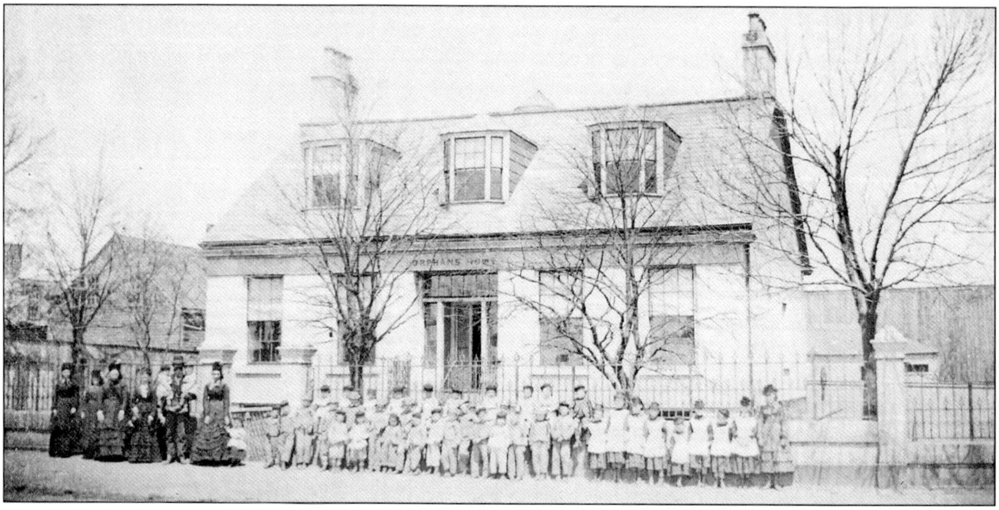

North Park Street was the location for this building, which housed the Protestant Orphans' Home, one of several orphanages in the city. The photograph was taken in May of 1874, and shows more than 30 children along with the staff of the orphanage. Note the interesting yet somewhat cumbersome uniforms! (Courtesy of the Photograph Collection, Public Archives of Nova Scotia, anonymous collection #5.)

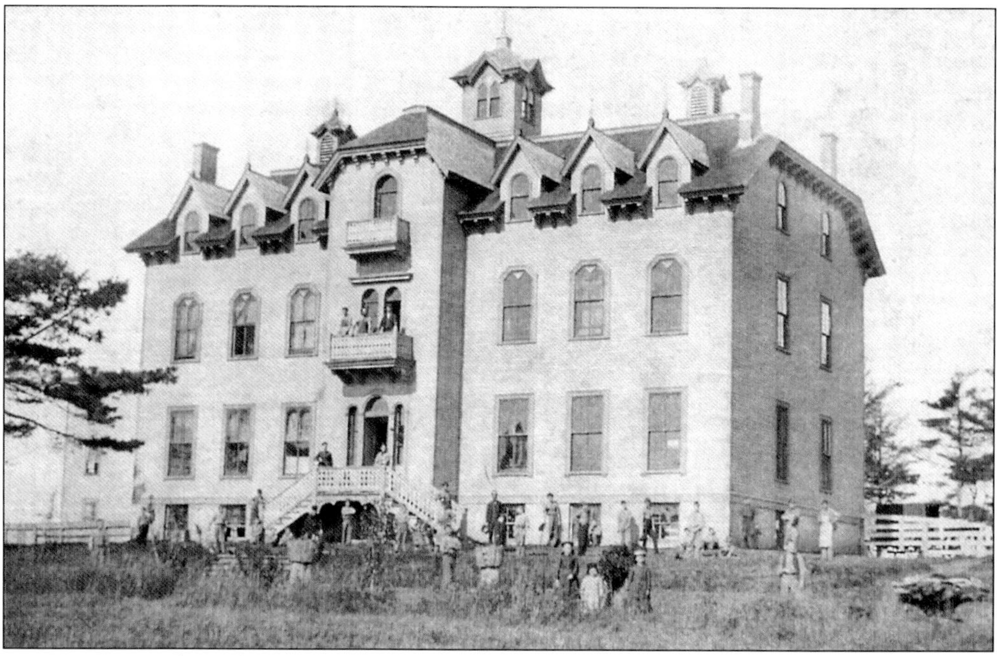

Set up in 1850, the Industrial School was known as the Ragged School. It moved to Quinpool Road from its Spring Garden location in 1871. In 1947 after being turned over to the government, it became the Nova Scotia School for Boys, and in addition, at that time the site also became the home to hundreds of houses. The days for the children were long—the *Halifax Reporter* of August 18, 1864 gave the schedule as, 6 a.m. rising, work from 7:15 to 6 p.m. with a one hour break, evening hours spent in school, and lights out at 10 p.m. (Courtesy of the Photograph Collection, Public Archives of Nova Scotia, United Church of Canada Committee on Archives 31.2.5.)

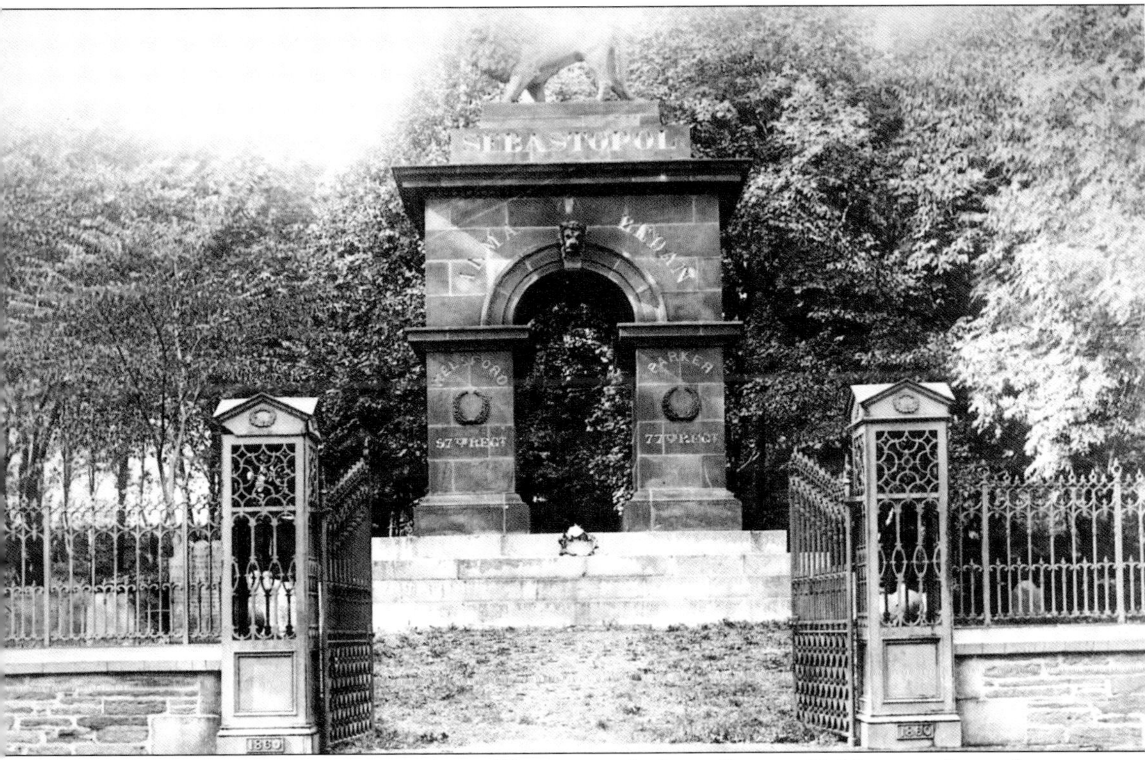

Because of its military position and its affiliations with Great Britain, Halifax was always front and centre of any wars which occurred. The Welsford-Parker Monument, otherwise known as the Sebastopol Monument, sits in the Old Burying Ground, the oldest cemetery in Halifax, which was in use from 1749 to 1843. The arch is a sandstone arch erected in 1860 commemorating the contributions made to the Crimean War of 1853–1856. Surprisingly, Halifax lost only two citizens to the conflict. (Courtesy of the Photograph Collection, Public Archives of Nova Scotia, Thomas Hill Collection, #24.)

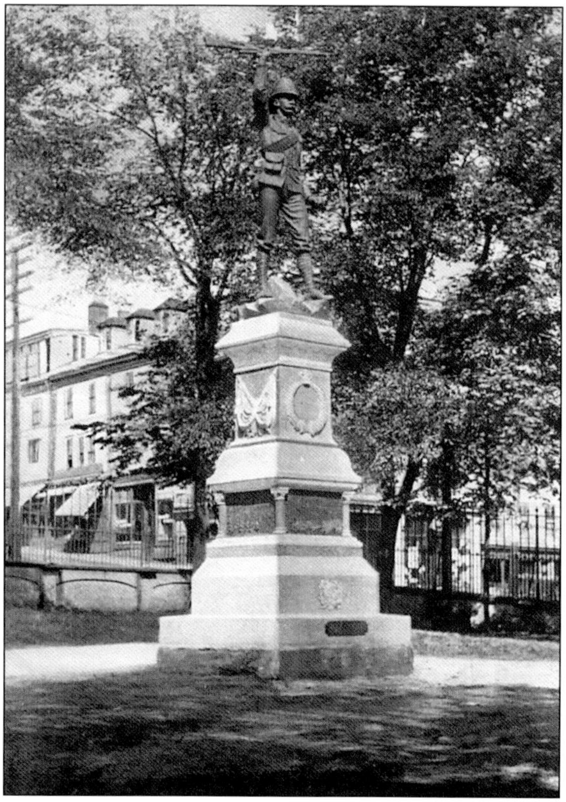

The Soldiers Monument in Provincial Square was raised in honour of the Boer War of October 11, 1899 to May 31, 1902 which saw all parts of the Empire rushing to South Africa. Many Haligonians went to the Deep Water Terminal to wave goodbye as the Canadians boarded the transport ship *Milwaukee*. Unlike the Crimean War before it, over a hundred Canadians were lost in the conflict.

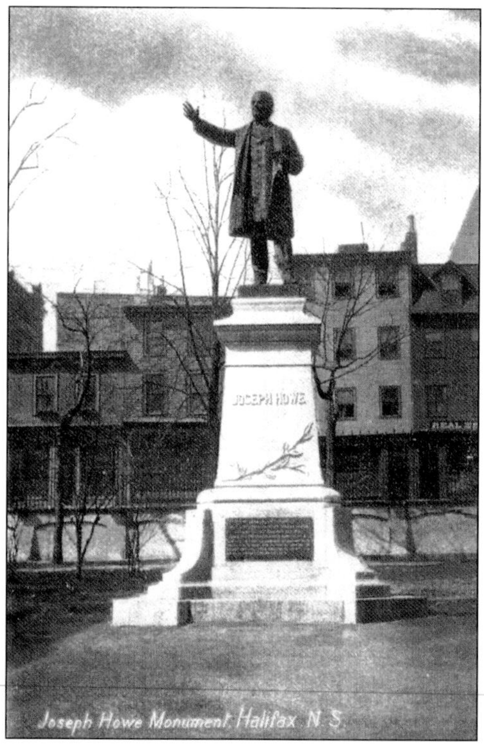

The Joseph Howe Monument also stands on Hollis Street. In 1836, Howe was elected to the Legislative Assembly. A champion of reform, Howe is considered to have been the founder of representative government in British North America. He was the Premier of the Province from 1860 to 1863.

Five

The Military

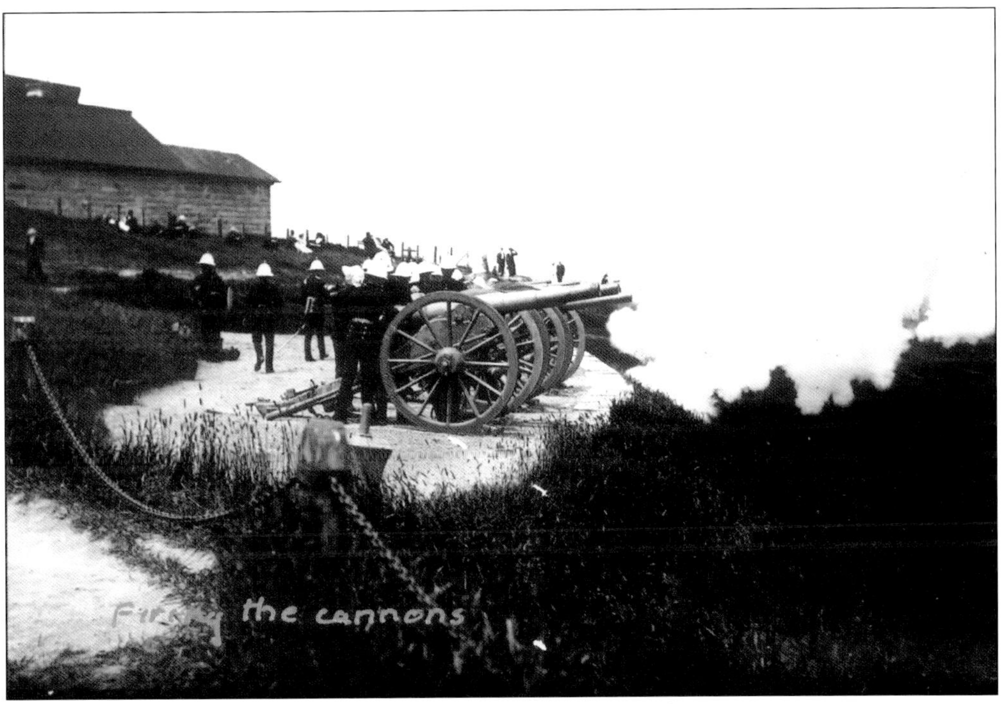

Pictured above is the firing of the cannons at the Citadel, Halifax.

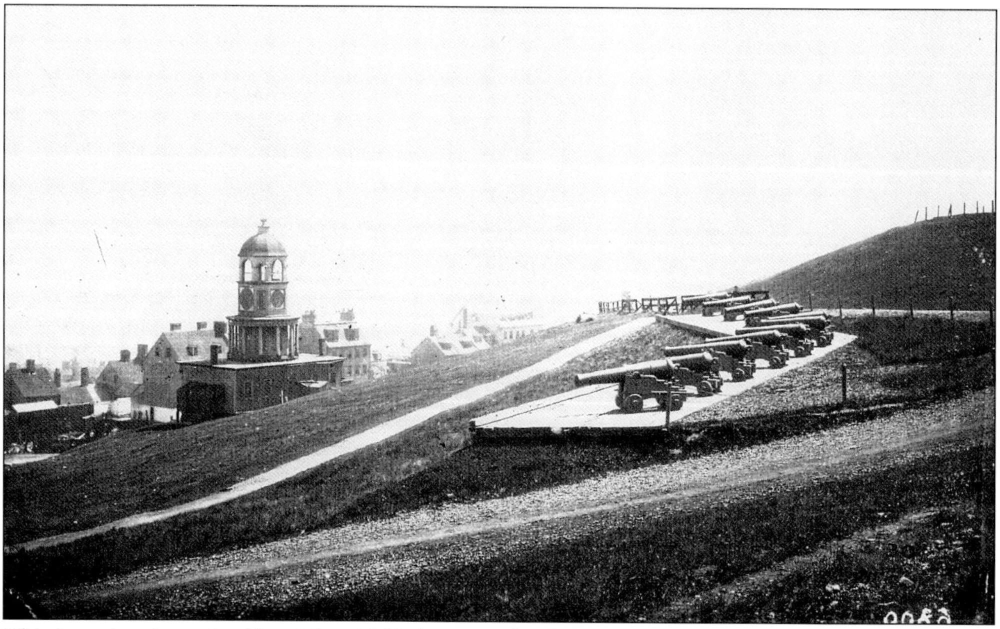

This is a view from the Citadel *c.* 1867 showing the Saluting Battery and the Town Clock. The Citadel was completed in 1856, but had been regularly fortified since around 1778. The cost of finishing the Citadel between 1828 and 1860 was over £33,800. The summit today is 80 feet lower than it had once been. (Courtesy of the Photograph Collection, Public Archives of Nova Scotia, Royal Engineers Collection, #30.)

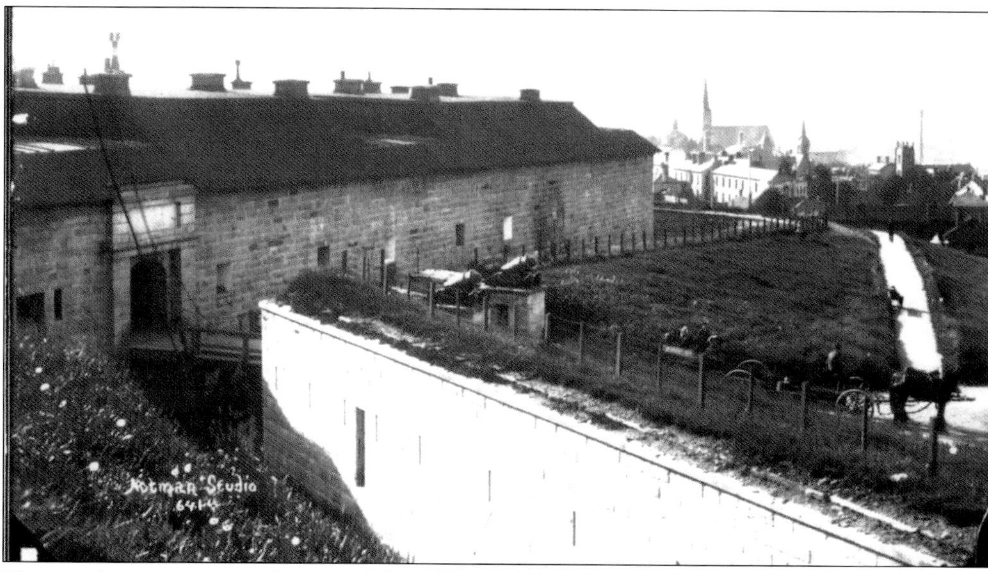

Here is the entrance to the Citadel and barracks taken from the inside wall *c.* 1900. The fortifications began with a single wooden wall in 1751. Work on the fortification began in earnest in the 1830s. In 1835, some of the 83rd Regiment were excavating a bank when it caved in, killing one man. In 1889, a fire at the Cavalier Barracks drew a crowd of thousands to the scene, until word spread that 300 tons of powder was only 40 feet away from the flames. (Courtesy of the Photograph Collection, Public Archives of Nova Scotia, Notman Collection #6414.)

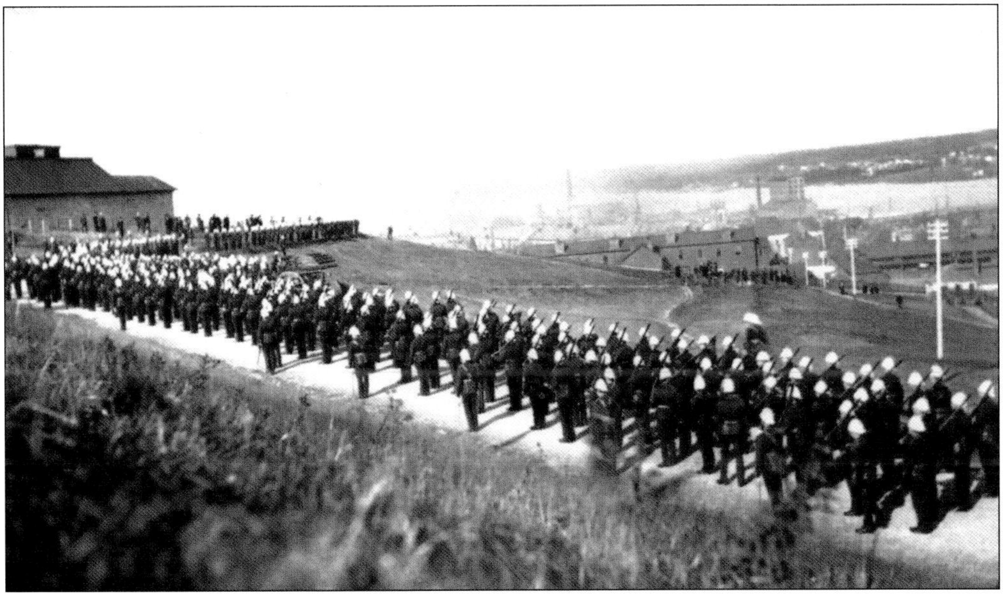

This is the Imperial Garrison outside of the Citadel, with an excellent view of the harbour. The guns and blockhouse on top of the hill were installed in 1775, and reconstructed by the Duke of Kent, father of Queen Victoria, in the late 1700s. In 1873, the *Acadian Recorder* announced that "people are denied the privilege of walking, sitting, standing on the Citadel Glacis because of a few cows which are quartered on the grounds in question, all access to this salubrious spot is forbidden to the people." (Courtesy of the Photograph Collection, Public Archives of Nova Scotia, J.A. Irvine Collection, Album #35, #7.)

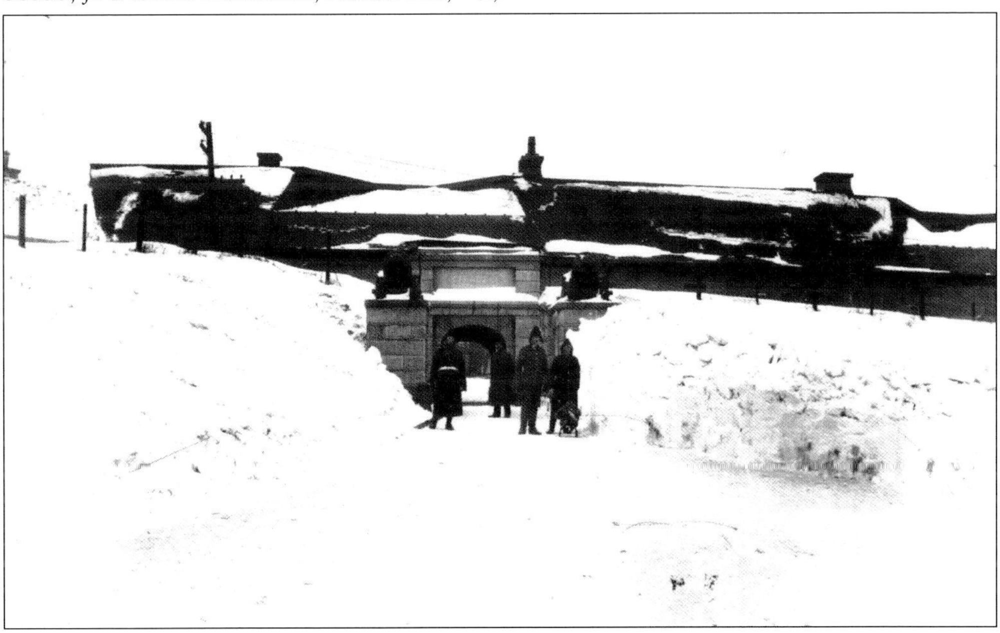

Pictured here is a winter scene on Citadel Hill, 1905. In March of 1917, a man on his way to Russia from New York was taken from a ship and detained at the Citadel for a short time, suspected of passport infringements. His name was Leon Trotsky. (Courtesy of the Photograph Collection, Public Archives of Nova Scotia, Notman Collection, #12662.)

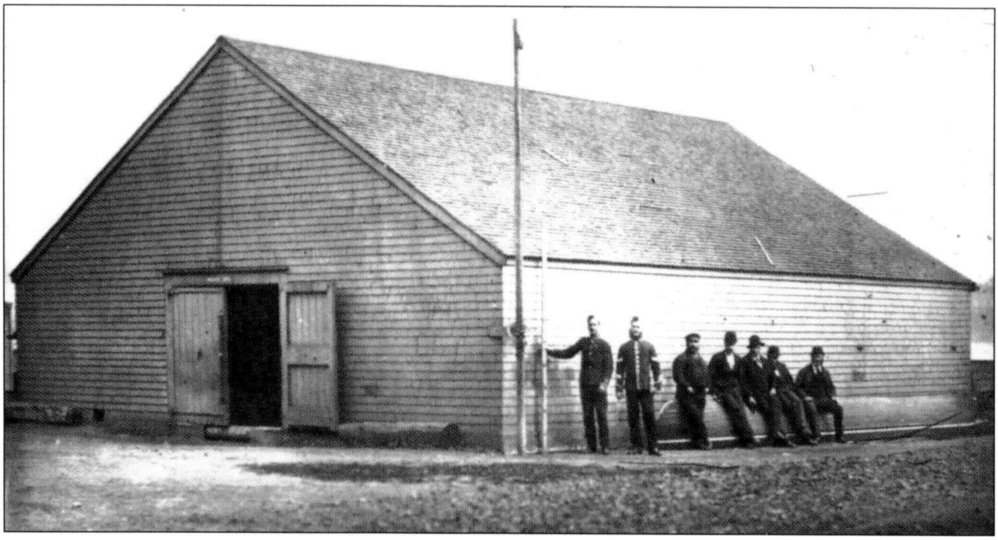

This is the Queens Wharf boat shed, photographed *c.* 1879. The Queens Wharf appeared on maps dating as far back as 1851. (Courtesy of the Photograph Collection, Public Archives of Nova Scotia, Royal Engineers Collection #243.)

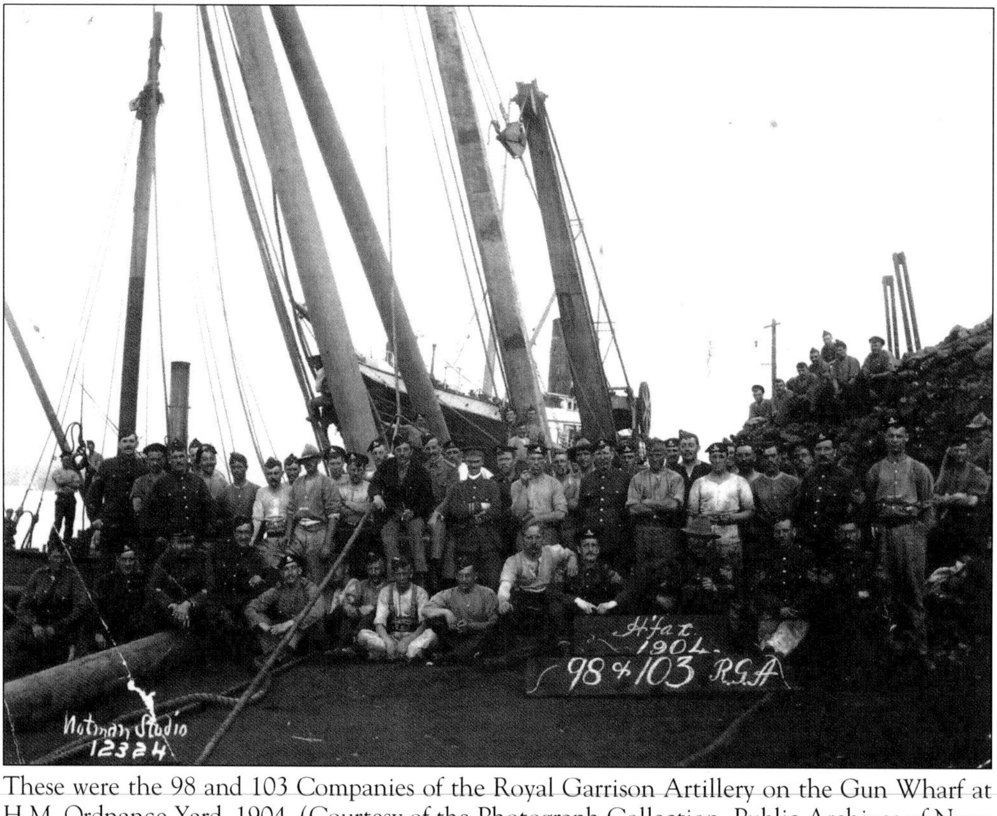

These were the 98 and 103 Companies of the Royal Garrison Artillery on the Gun Wharf at H.M. Ordnance Yard, 1904. (Courtesy of the Photograph Collection, Public Archives of Nova Scotia, Notman Collection, #12324.)

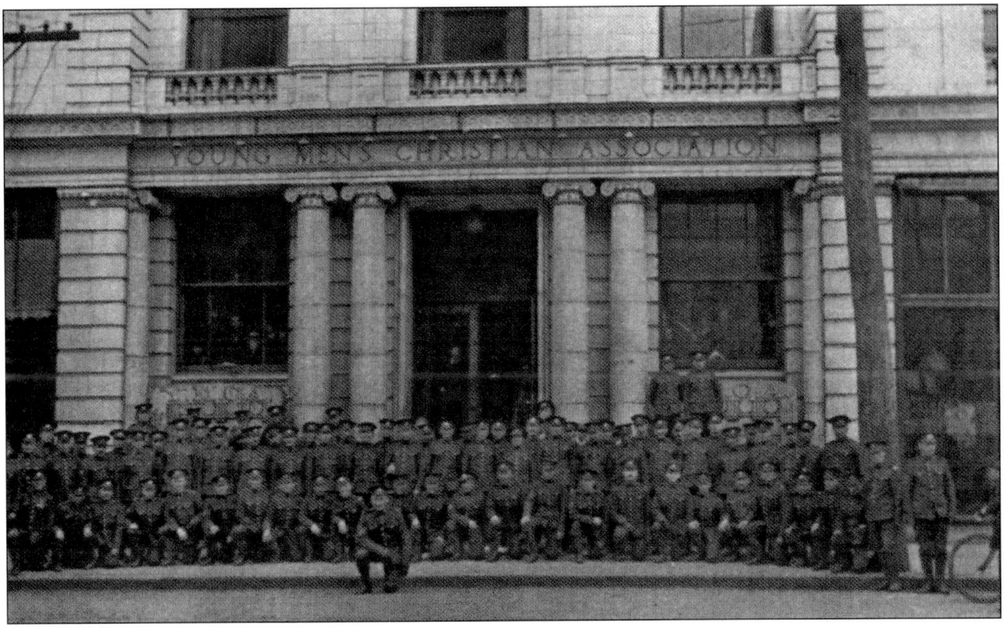

A group of soldiers during the 1910 decade pose for a group photograph outside the YMCA building on Barrington Street. (Courtesy of the Photograph Collection, Public Archives of Nova Scotia, Arthur Bloomfield Dawson fonds, series 1, #1500.)

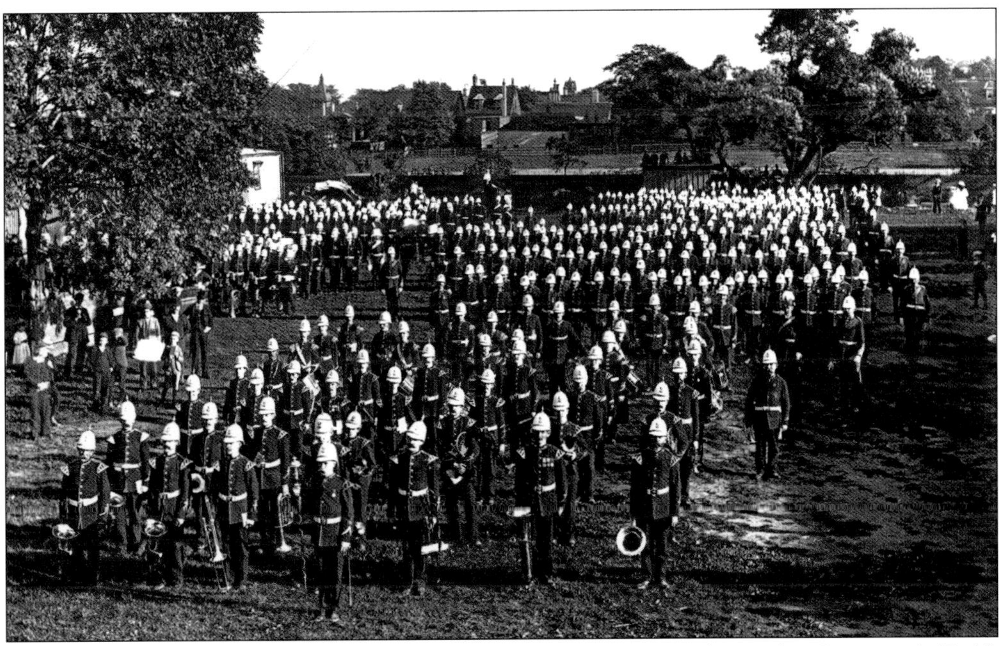

Pictured here are the Princess Louise Fusiliers c. 1885 on parade in the Governor's Field, between Barrington and Queen Streets with Morris Street running across the top of the picture. The site is now home to the Nova Scotia Technical College on Spring Garden Road. (Courtesy of the Photograph Collection, Public Archives of Nova Scotia, anonymous oversize collection #33.)

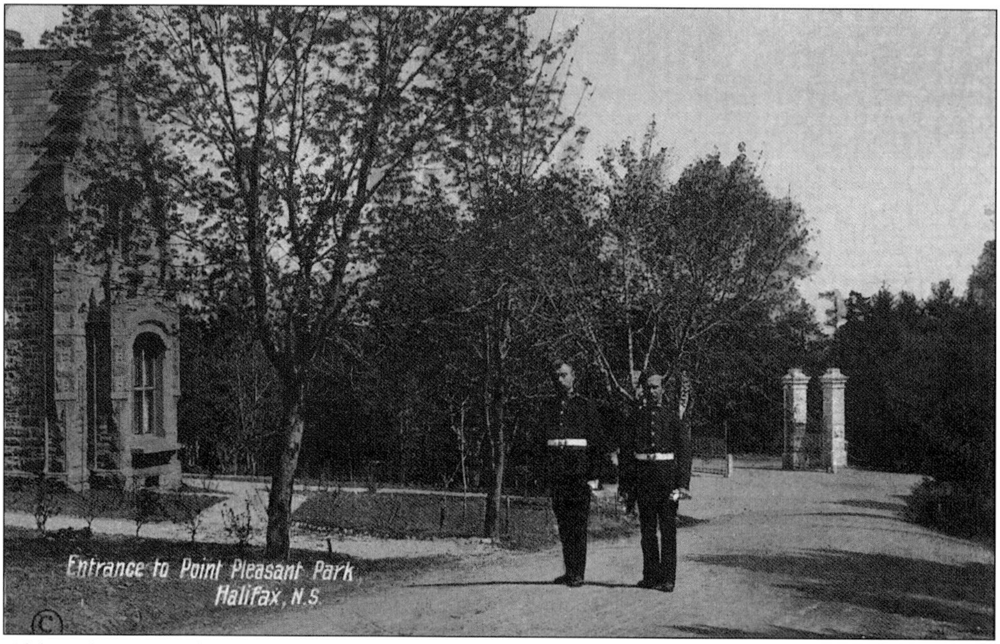

Although it is and was (as of 1873) a park, Point Pleasant also housed a number of military buildings. Cornwallis had chosen this southernmost tip as the site for the city which became Halifax because of its defensibility, but the gales and rocky shore moved it farther north. However, several batteries, Fort Ogilvie, and the Prince of Wales Tower gave the area a distinctly military flavour.

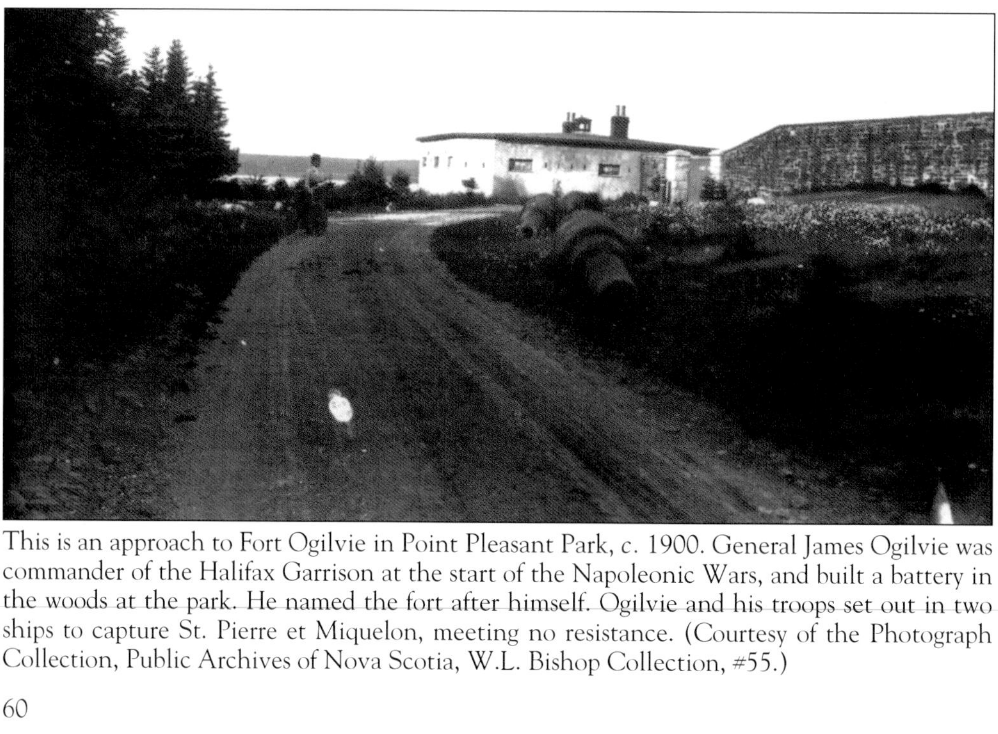

This is an approach to Fort Ogilvie in Point Pleasant Park, c. 1900. General James Ogilvie was commander of the Halifax Garrison at the start of the Napoleonic Wars, and built a battery in the woods at the park. He named the fort after himself. Ogilvie and his troops set out in two ships to capture St. Pierre et Miquelon, meeting no resistance. (Courtesy of the Photograph Collection, Public Archives of Nova Scotia, W.L. Bishop Collection, #55.)

Six

The Sea

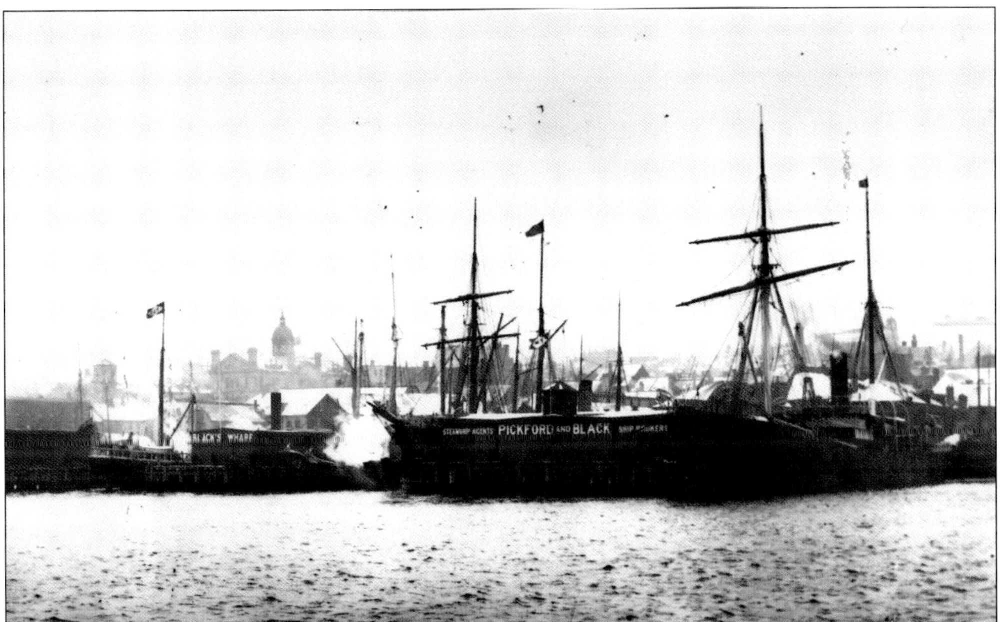

Seen here is the waterfront showing the Pickford & Black wharf. (Courtesy of the Photograph Collection, Public Archives of Nova Scotia, Notman Collection, #70651.)

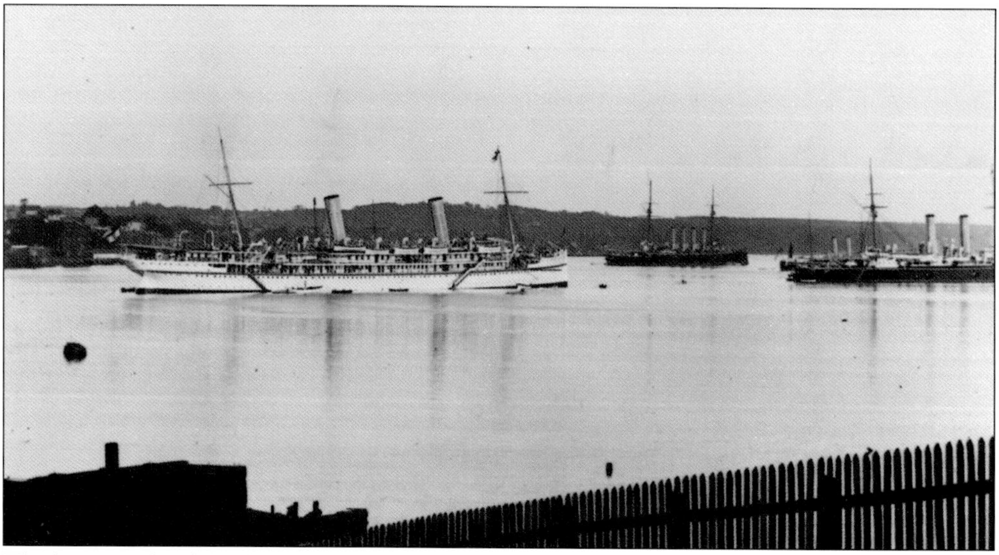

The history of Halifax leans heavily upon the sea. Many of the docks lay in the North End of the city, however, this picture was taken from H.M. Ordnance Yard, farther south along the waterfront. This shows H.M. Royal Yacht Ophir in October 1901, with an escort of ships, including from left to right, the H.M.S. *Diadem* and the H.M.S. *Crescent*. (Courtesy of the Photograph Collection, Public Archives of Nova Scotia, W.L. Bishop Collection #65.)

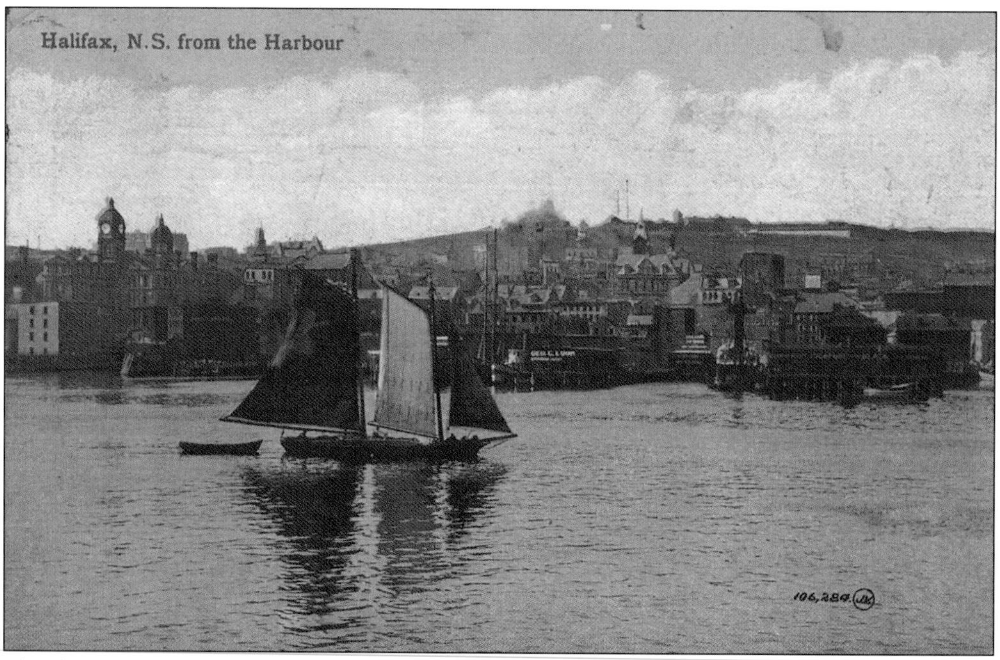

The downtown of Halifax along with the Geo. C. Cook (centre) and Pickford and Black (right) wharves can be seen on this turn-of-the-century postcard of the waterfront.

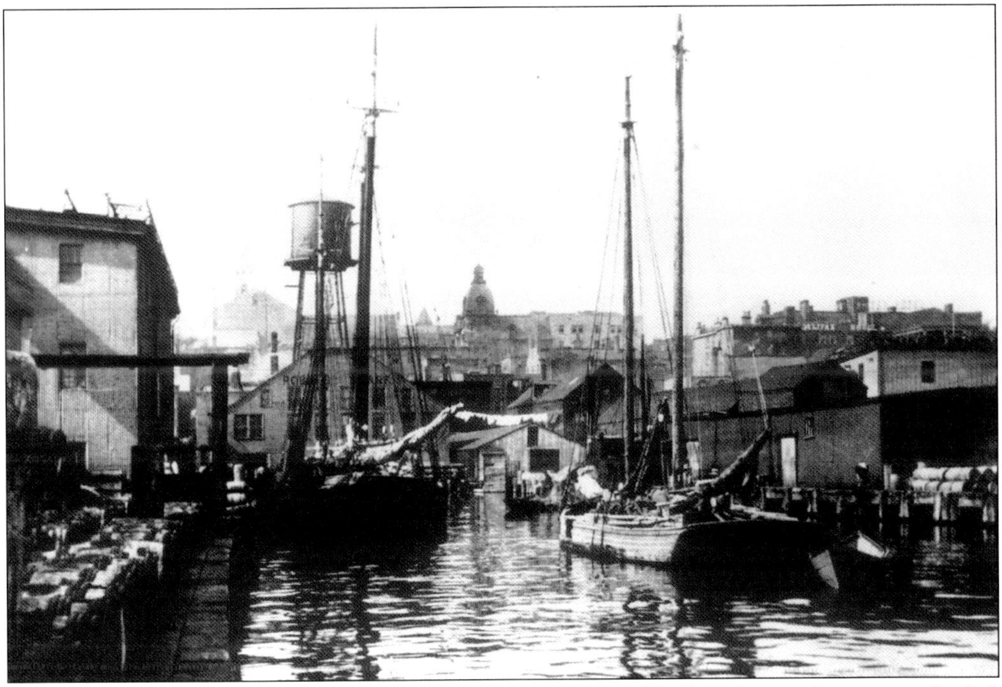

Pictured above is the waterfront taken *c.* 1920. St. Mary's Church spire can be seen to the left of the picture, and, over the buildings on the right, the top of the Halifax Hotel on Hollis Street is clearly visible.

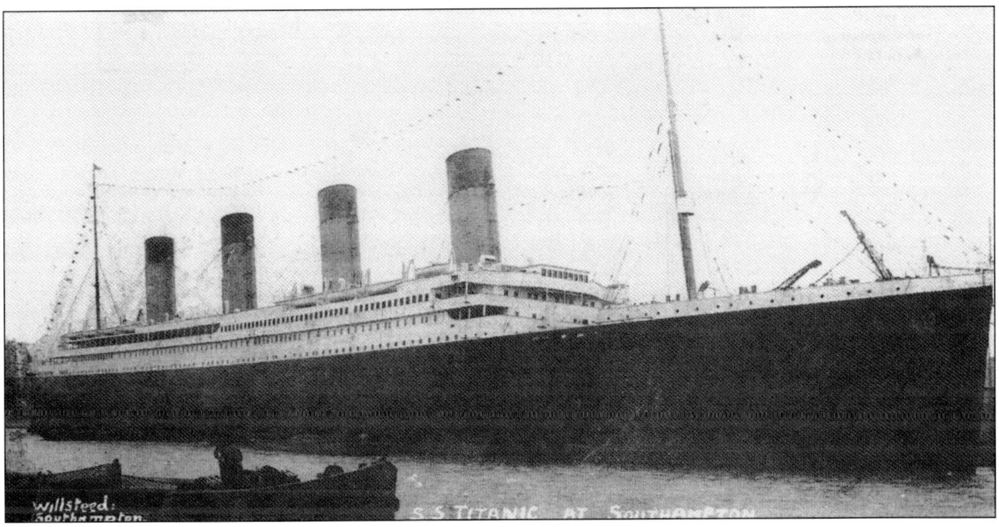

The sea knows no boundaries, and so South End and North End blur when faced with such a disaster as the loss of the S.S. *Titanic*. This picture of the ill-fated White Star Line vessel was taken in Southampton prior to its maiden voyage in April 1912. Many hundreds of vessels have found watery graves around Halifax, and although the *Titanic* went down off Newfoundland, the whole of Halifax was front and centre in the rescue attempt. Many victims of the disaster are buried in the city.

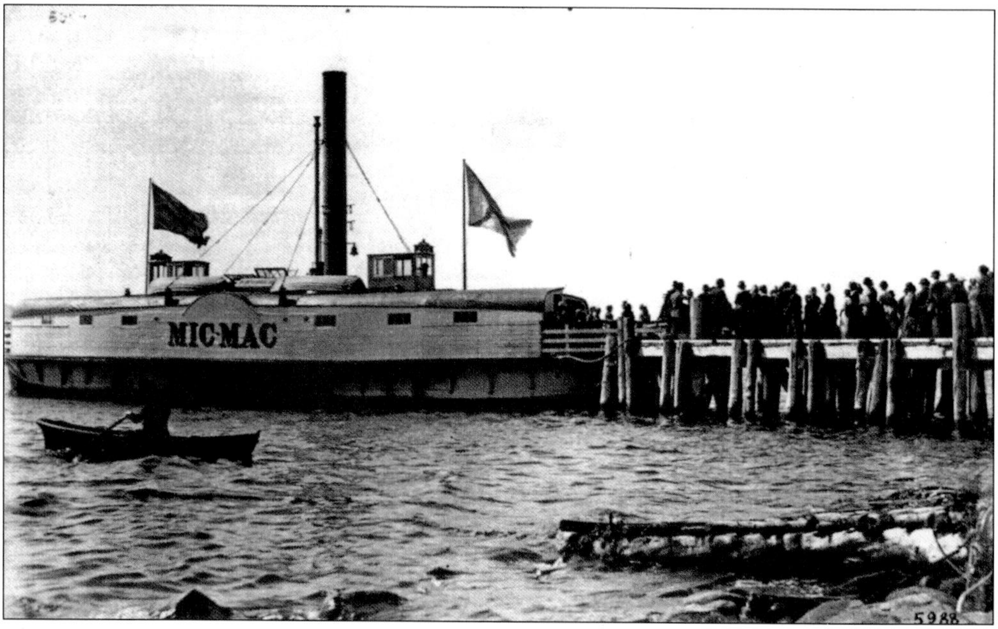

The history of crossing between Dartmouth and Halifax is a storied one. The first ferryman was John Connor, and the first ferry sailed between the two fledgling towns in December of 1751. By 1815, the ferry trip was down to 40 minutes, and ran on a "once it's full we're going" basis. Arrival was signaled by a conch shell. In 1816, a team boat with eight horses cut the time down to 20 minutes. These pictures show the ferry steamers. The top picture is the steamer Mic-Mac, built in 1844 at wharf at the Mt. Hope Insane Asylum in Dartmouth, with a picnic party, c. 1885. In spite of two bridges crossing the Narrows, ferries continue to unite the cities. (Top: courtesy of the Photograph Collection, Public Archives of Nova Scotia, G.L. Sinclair Collection, #4; bottom: courtesy of the Photograph Collection, Public Archives of Nova Scotia, J.A. Irvine Collection, Album #37, #138.)

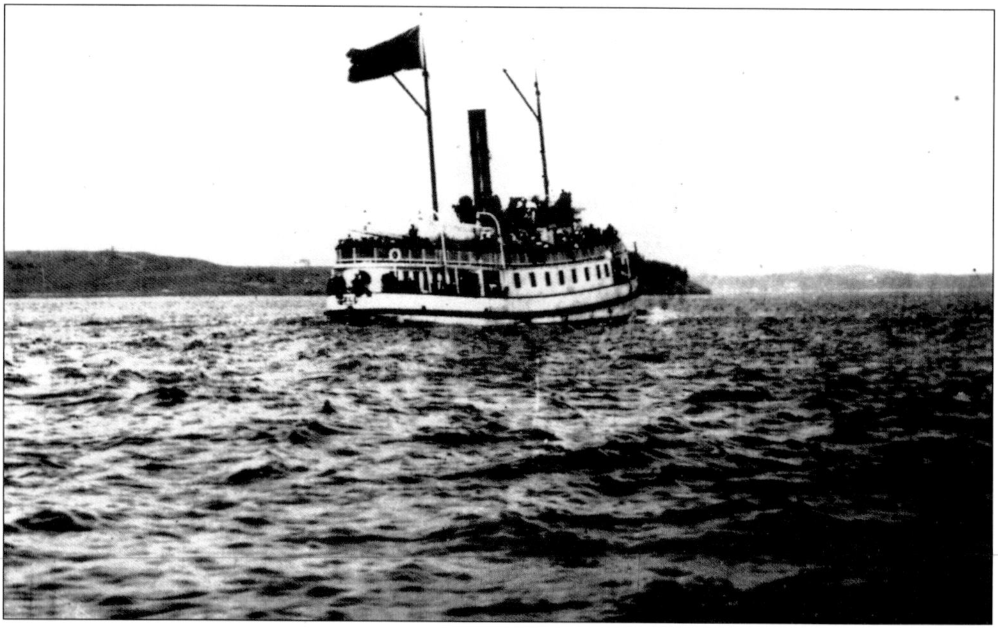

Seven

PEOPLE

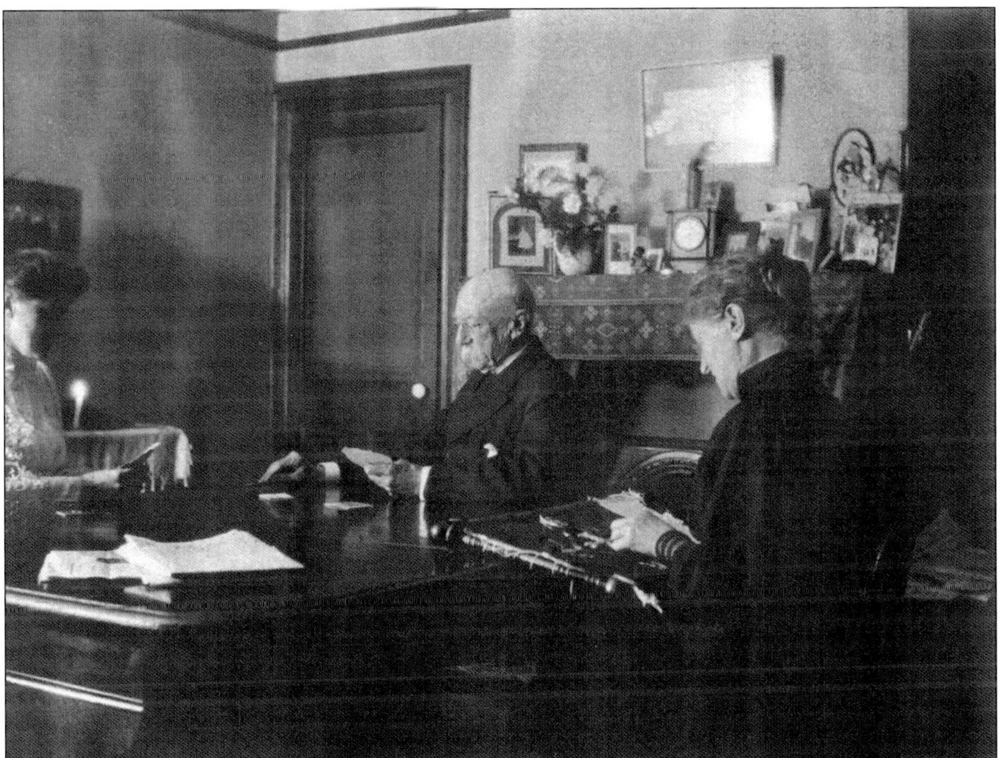

Seen here are Edmund Dockett Tucker, Esq., founder of Snow Co. Ltd., with Mrs. Eliza Ann Tucker and Miss Mary Tucker, taken at Pine Grove, Bower Road, before 1912. (Courtesy of the Photograph Collection, Public Archives of Nova Scotia, K.W. Wainwright Collection, #1.)

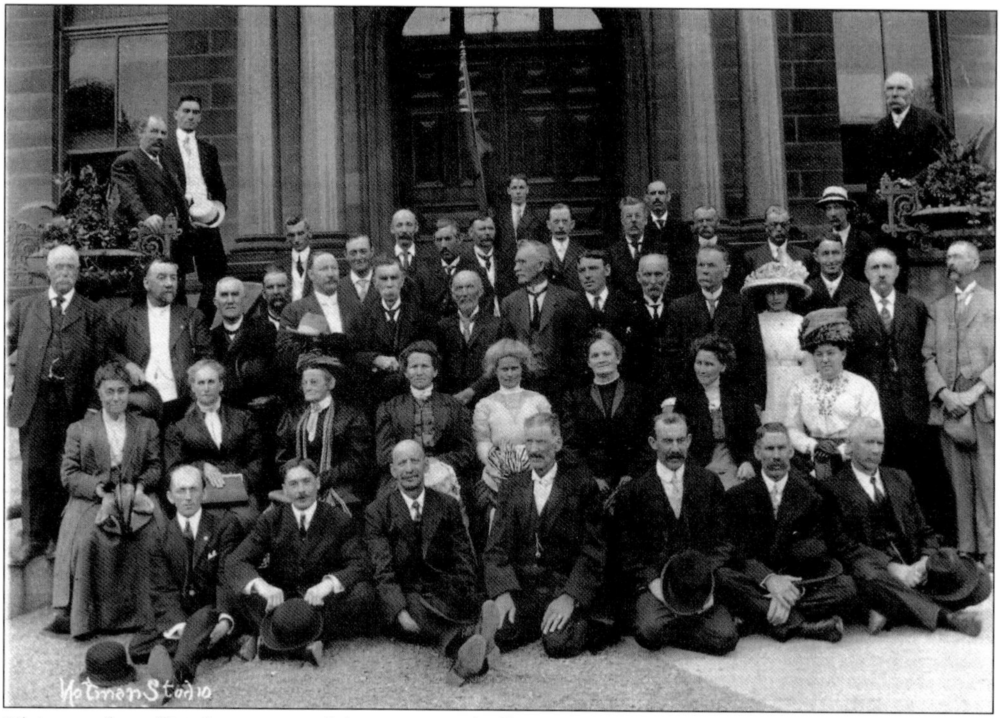

This was the official opening of the new city hall in 1890. The only threat to the new building came not from the Halifax Explosion but from a riot in May of 1918, when a sailor was arrested for shoplifting on Barrington Street. The disturbance grew until the police retreated into the city hall and part of the throng broke in and destroyed everything in sight. (Courtesy of the Photograph Collection, Public Archives of Nova Scotia, Notman Collection, #20220.)

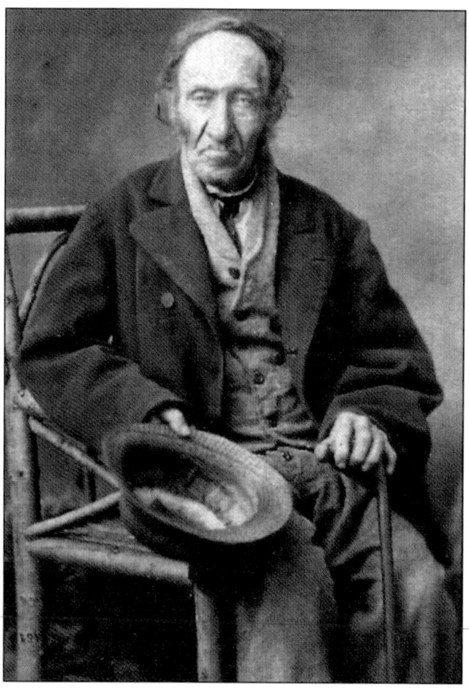

One of the familiar faces around Halifax for over half a century was that of William (Jock) Craig, who was the letter carrier for the General Post Office for 54 years. The picture was taken August 1, 1871, when Jock was a sprightly 81 years old. (Courtesy of the Photograph Collection, Public Archives of Nova Scotia, Notman Collection, #6248.)

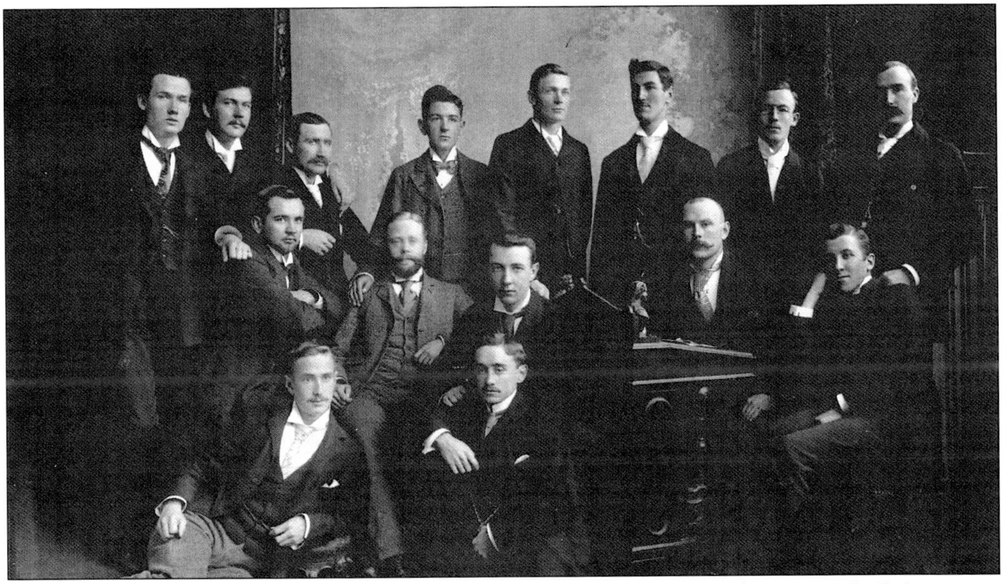

Some of the doctors in the photographs of Victoria General Hospital in 1910 doubtless arose from this group of gentlemen. The Third Year Medical Class at Dalhousie University was photographed in 1895. Note the distinct lack of potential female doctors. (Courtesy of the Photograph Collection, Public Archives of Nova Scotia, Notman Collection, #2396.)

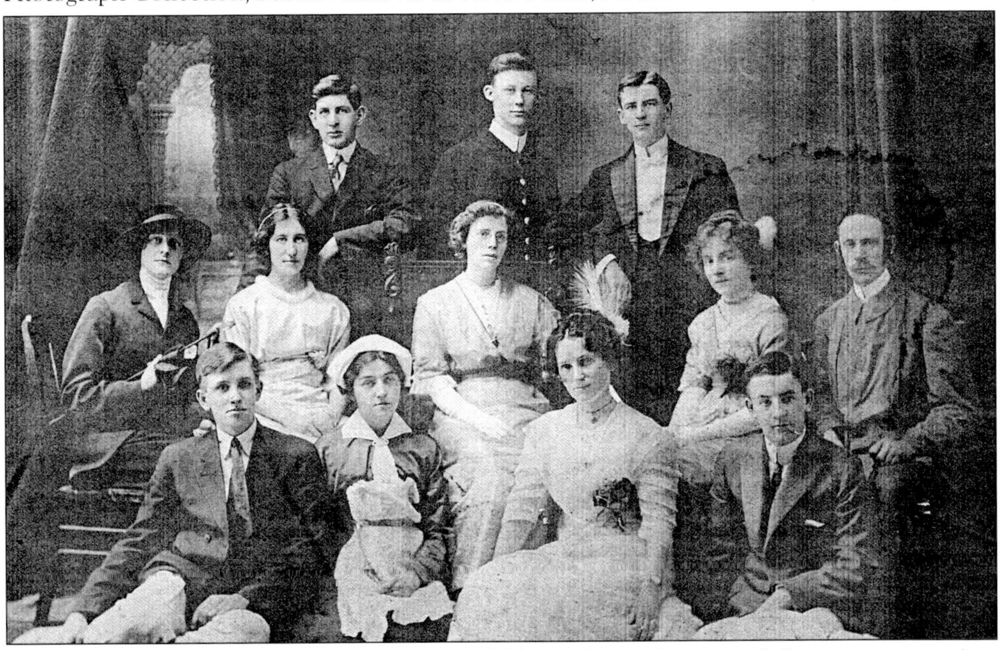

One of the few forms of entertainment available in the early years of this century was live theatre. This group, the Park Street Dramatic Club, are dressed for the play they were performing, which was their 1914 production entitled *A Scrap of Paper*. Pictured from left to right are: (front row) A. Greig, A. Burns, F. Thompson, and W. Scriven; (centre row) M. McColl, E. Stewart, L. Mitchell, E. Gibson, and L. Wallis; (back row) W. Lucas, H. O'Brien, and W. Stewart. (Courtesy of the Photograph Collection, Public Archives of Nova Scotia, C.H. Climo Collection, #7.)

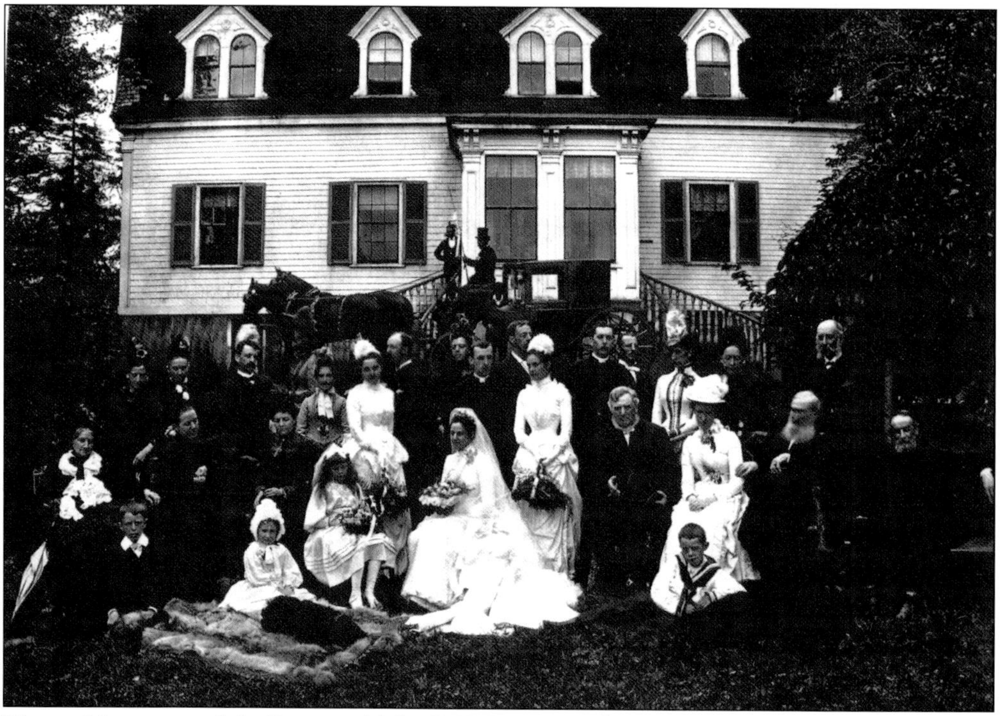

The wedding party of the Reverend John E.H. Binney and Miss Beatrice E.L. Almon assembled on the lawn of Rosebank, 163 Jubilee Road, on September 4, 1888. (Courtesy of the Photograph Collection, Public Archives of Nova Scotia, Notman Collection, #65816.)

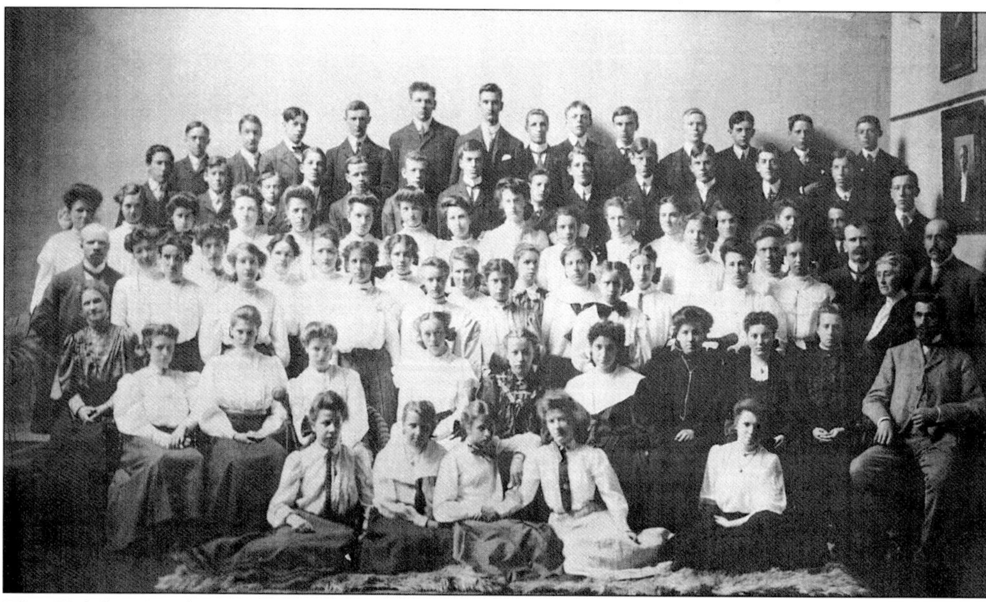

The Halifax Academy was founded in 1789. The cornerstone for their new location was laid in 1878 at the corner of Brunswick and Sackville Streets. Girls were admitted in 1885. This picture shows the Graduating Class of 1906. The last class to graduate came out of the school in 1942. (Courtesy of the Photograph Collection, Public Archives of Nova Scotia, Gauvin & Gentzell Collection, #36, #40-1.)

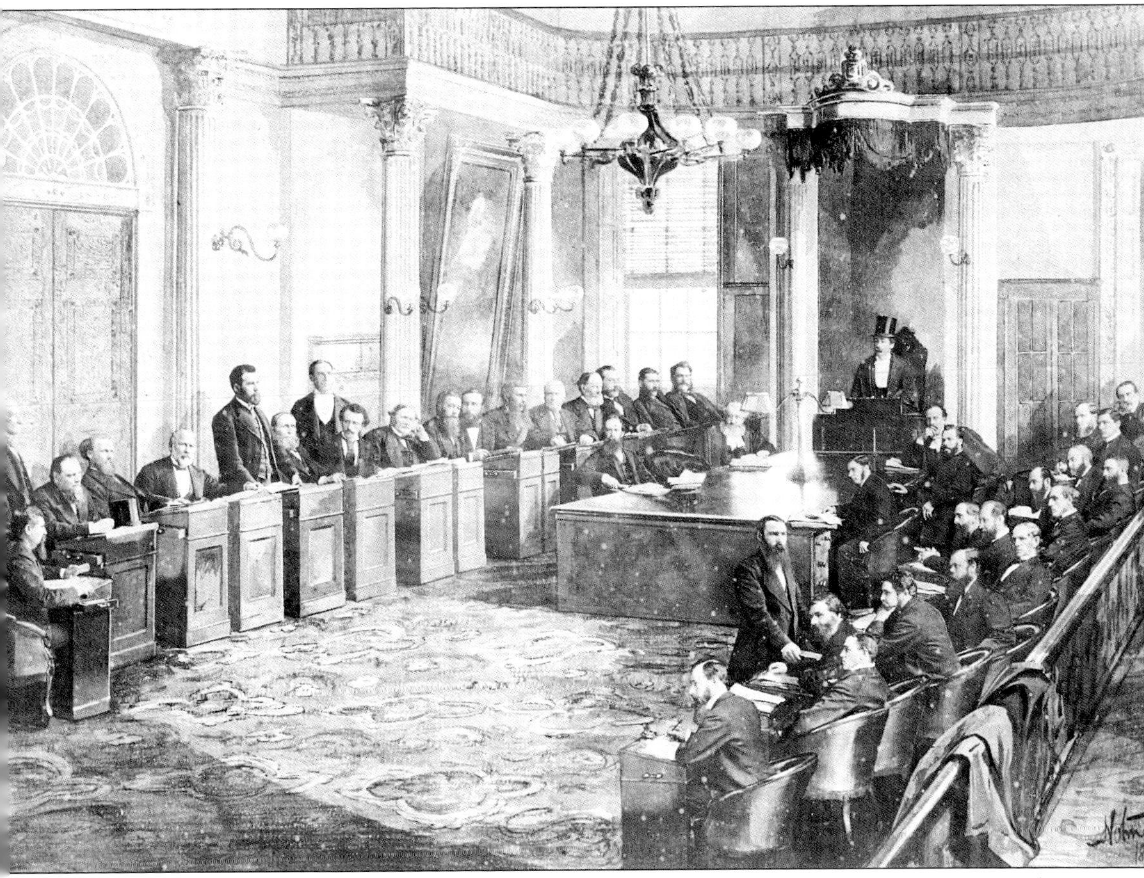

This is the Assembly Chamber before the east and west ends were made into offices in the time of Premier W.S. Fielding, at Province House, 1879, 60 years after the legislature met in the building for the first time. Until 1862 the Supreme Court also held its sessions in Province House, but moved in that year to their new building on Spring Garden Road. Charles Dickens witnessed the opening of the legislature here in 1842, and described it as, "like looking at Westminster through the wrong end of the telescope." The beautiful building still stands today and serves as a reminder of the history it created in 1848 as the first responsible government outside of Britain in the British Empire. (Courtesy of the Photograph Collection, Public Archives of Nova Scotia, N.S. House of Assembly Collection, #6, #34-32.)

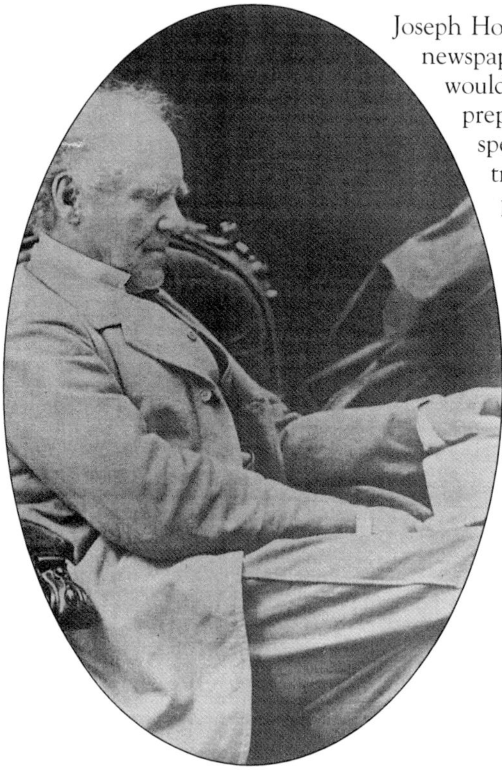

Joseph Howe in 1865, was the editor of the *Novascotian* newspaper, and was sued for libel in 1834. No lawyer would take on the case, so Howe hit the books and prepared his own defense. After a famous six-hour speech, he was acquitted. A year after the 1835 trial, Howe immersed himself in politics and political reform. After a wonderful career, he became lieutenant governor of Nova Scotia in 1873, yet died after only three weeks in office. (Courtesy of the Photograph Collection, Public Archives of Nova Scotia, anon. oversize collection, #2.)

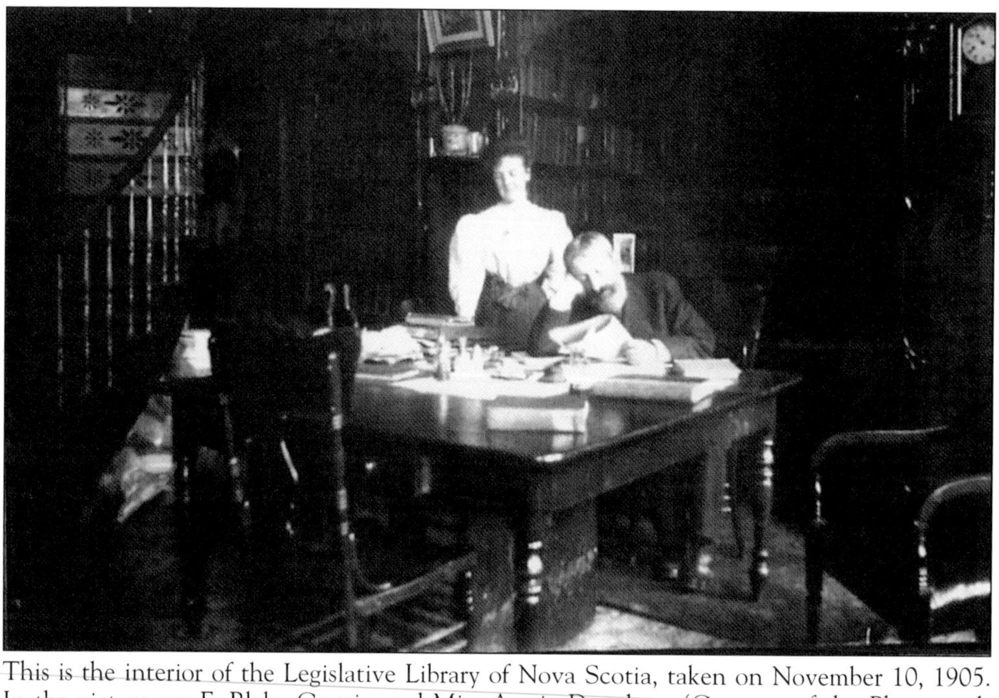

This is the interior of the Legislative Library of Nova Scotia, taken on November 10, 1905. In the picture are F. Blake Crettin and Miss Annie Donahue. (Courtesy of the Photograph Collection, Public Archives of Nova Scotia, C.E. Smith Collection, #14.)

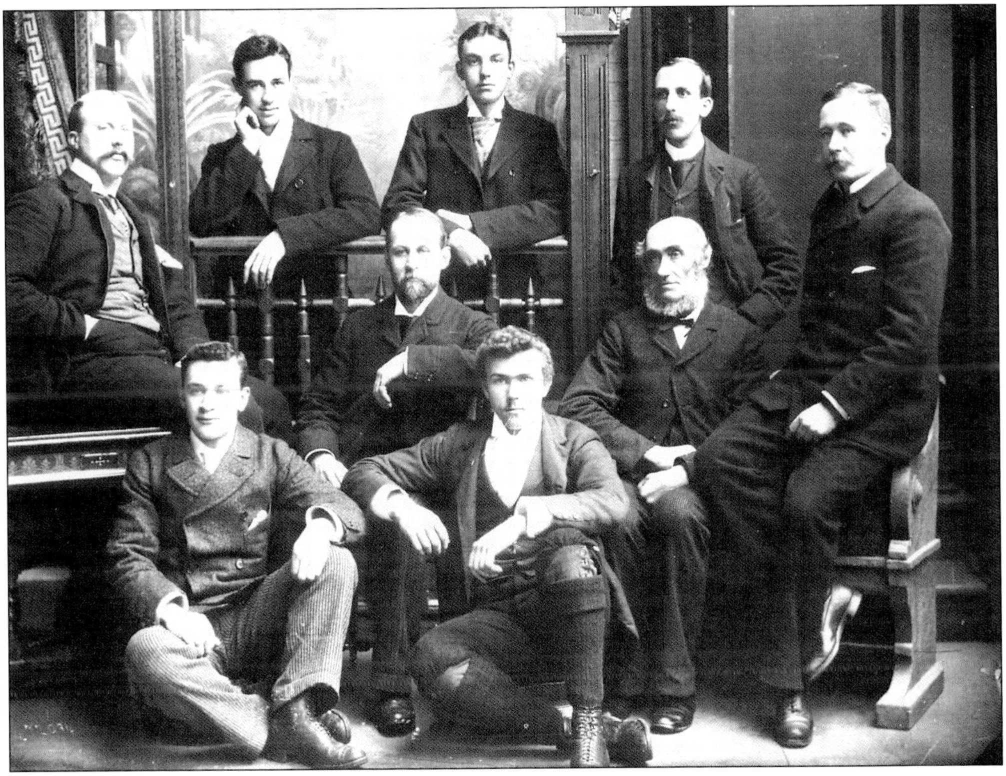

After the war of 1815, a depression set in, and businessman Enos Collins began a private banking business in part of a warehouse at 53-55 Upper Water Street. The business expanded and Halifax's first bank, the Halifax Banking Company was established in 1825. The bank used the premises until 1903, and remained there for five more years after amalgamating with the Canadian Imperial Bank of Commerce. This picture shows the Halifax Banking Company group c. 1892. (Courtesy of the Photograph Collection, Public Archives of Nova Scotia, Notman Collection #72034-15.)

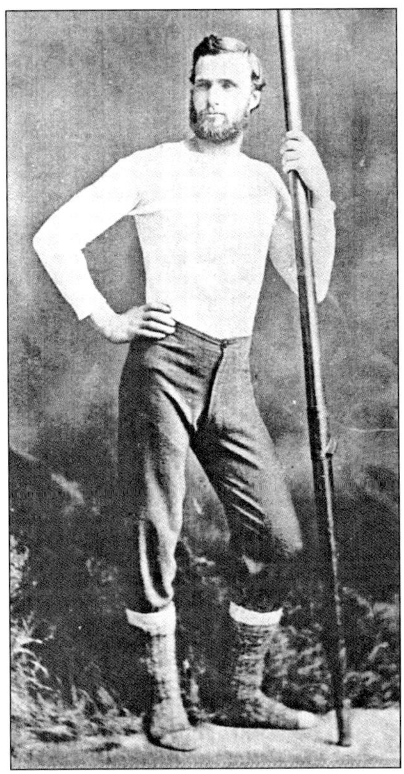

One of the most famous figures in Halifax in the mid-19th century was George Brown, the "Champion Oarsman of the World." Born at Herring Cove, NS, on February 7, 1839, he lived to only 36 years of age. His first appearance was at the age of 24 in a contest in Halifax Harbour. (Courtesy of the Photograph Collection, Public Archives of Nova Scotia, Tom Connors Old Sport #211.)

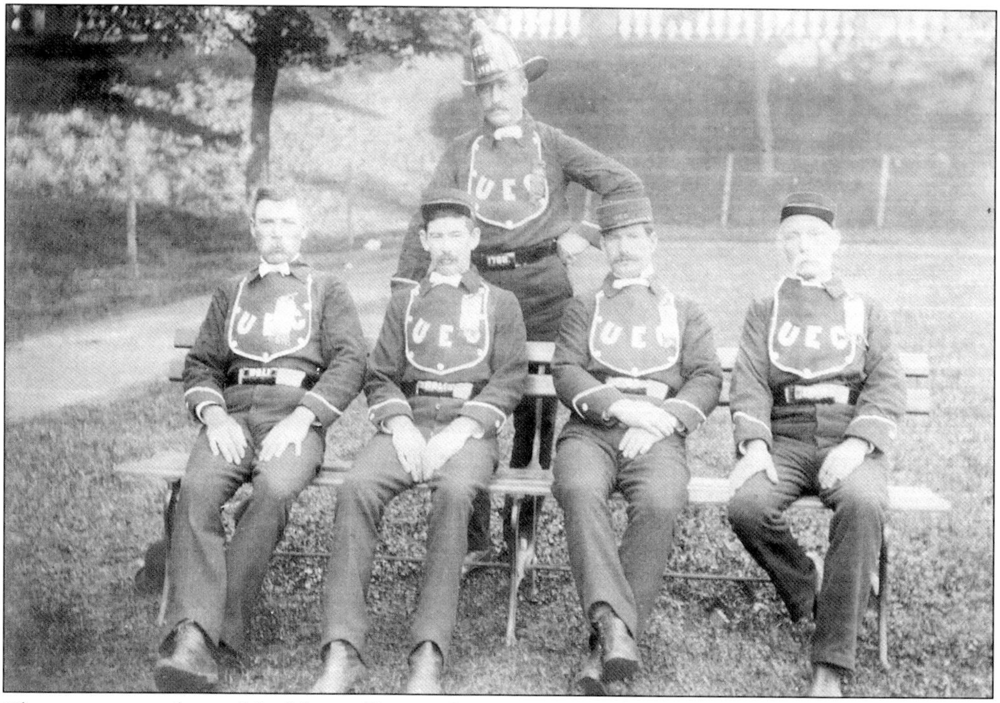

These were members of the Union Engine Company, Grand Parade *c.* 1900. The first volunteer fire company in Halifax was probably the Sun Fire Company, set up around 1801. Other companies sprang up including the Phoenix, the Hand-in-Hand, and the Heart-in-Hand. As well as being firefighting units they were also clubs. Paid, part-time firemen were first employed by the city in 1894. (Courtesy of the Photograph Collection, Public Archives of Nova Scotia, Don Cunningham Collection 33-4-1.)

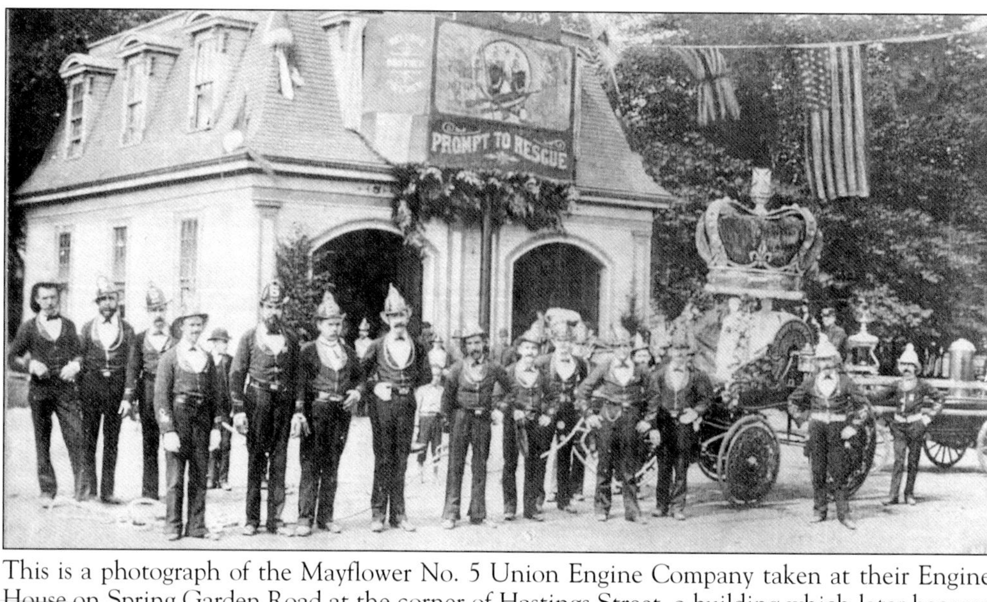

This is a photograph of the Mayflower No. 5 Union Engine Company taken at their Engine House on Spring Garden Road at the corner of Hastings Street, a building which later became Connolly's Book Store. The photograph was taken at the August 10, 1886 carnival. (Courtesy of the Photograph Collection, Public Archives of Nova Scotia, Tom Connors Old Sport #648.)

Eight

Events

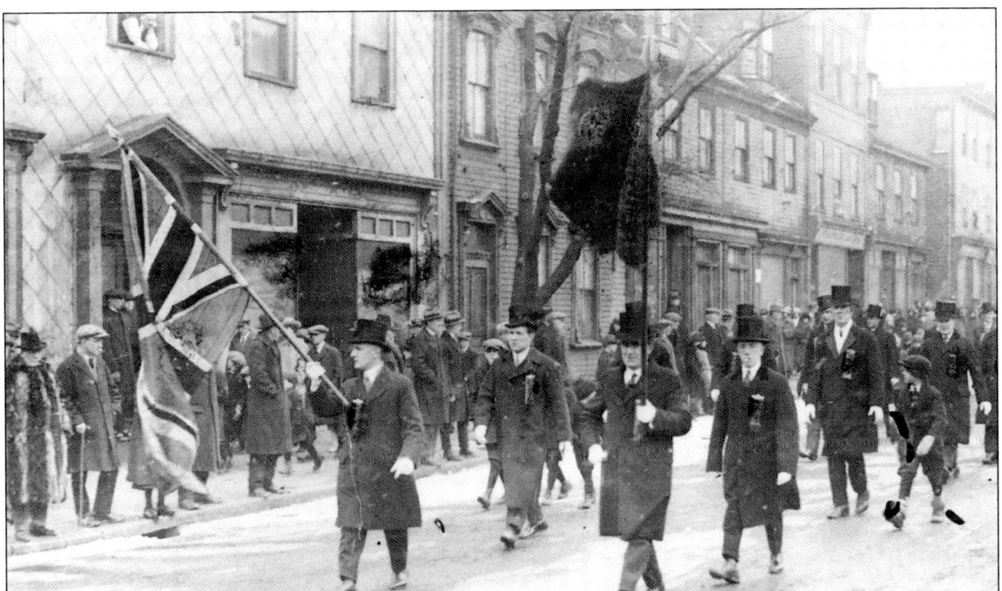

An early St. Patrick's Day (March 17) Parade, including the Charitable Irish Society, formed in 1786. (Courtesy of the Photograph Collection, Public Archives of Nova Scotia, PANS N-3808.)

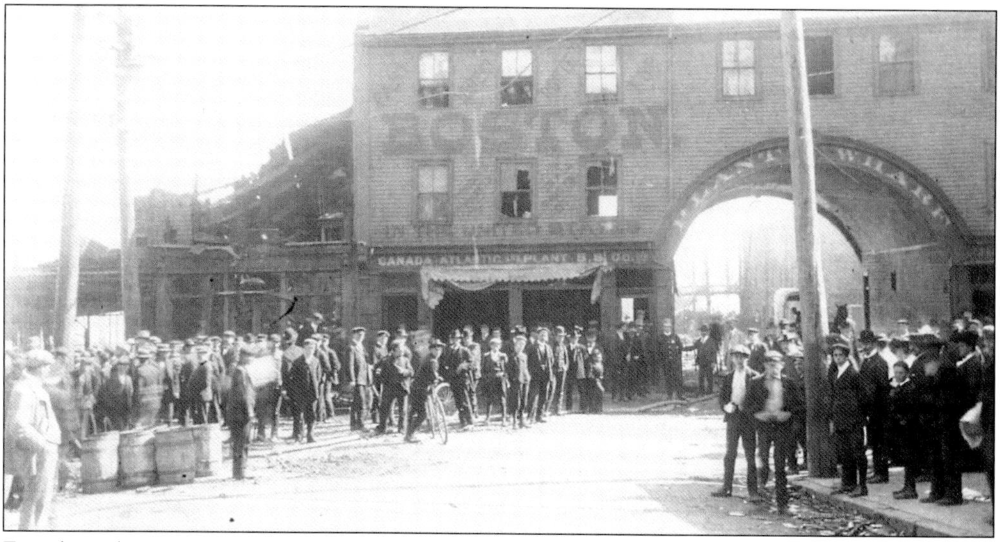

Fires have been prevalent throughout Halifax's 250-year history. This shows the aftermath of the fire at T.J. Egan's Gunshop and Sporting Goods Store, Lower Water Street, c. 1903, with the Plant Line Offices and Arch (later the Irving Arch) to the right. On May 29, 1874, the *Acadian Recorder* noted that "Egan's in Halifax purchased 2,200 guns of various patterns from New Brunswick Arsenal, some stamped *Potsdam Magazine*, which must have been brought by Hessian soldiers who fought in the American Revolution." (Courtesy of the Photograph Collection, Public Archives of Nova Scotia, Thomas W. Chisholm Collection, #1.)

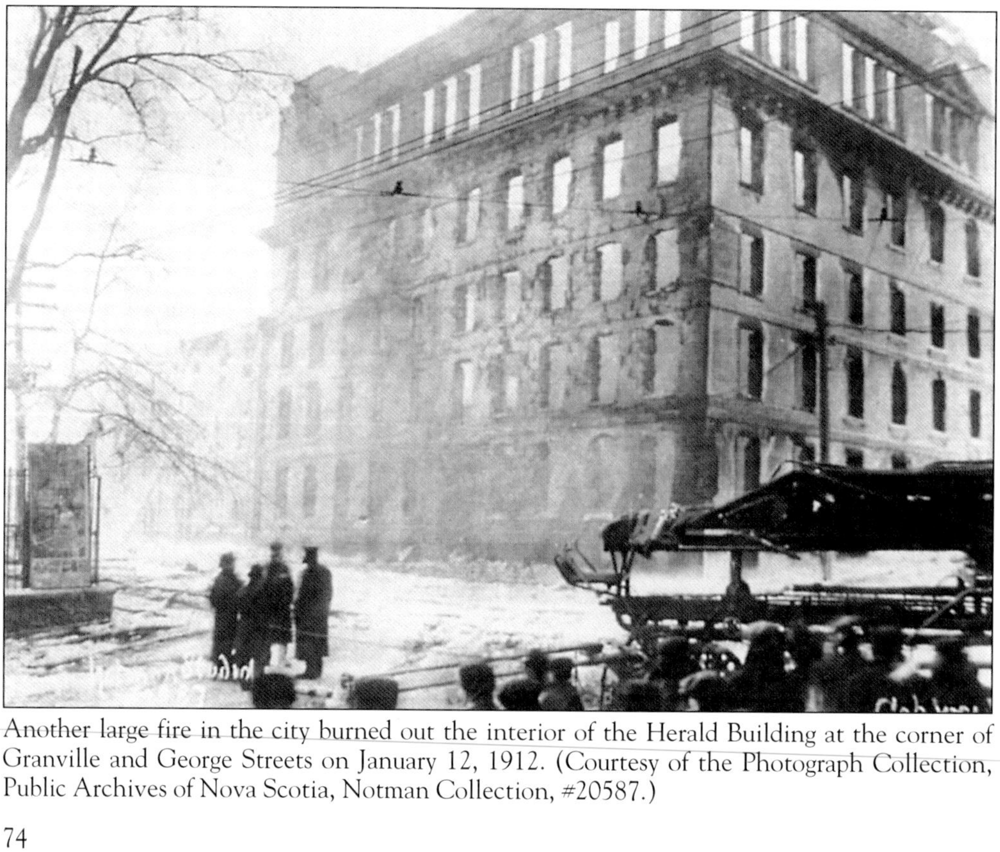

Another large fire in the city burned out the interior of the Herald Building at the corner of Granville and George Streets on January 12, 1912. (Courtesy of the Photograph Collection, Public Archives of Nova Scotia, Notman Collection, #20587.)

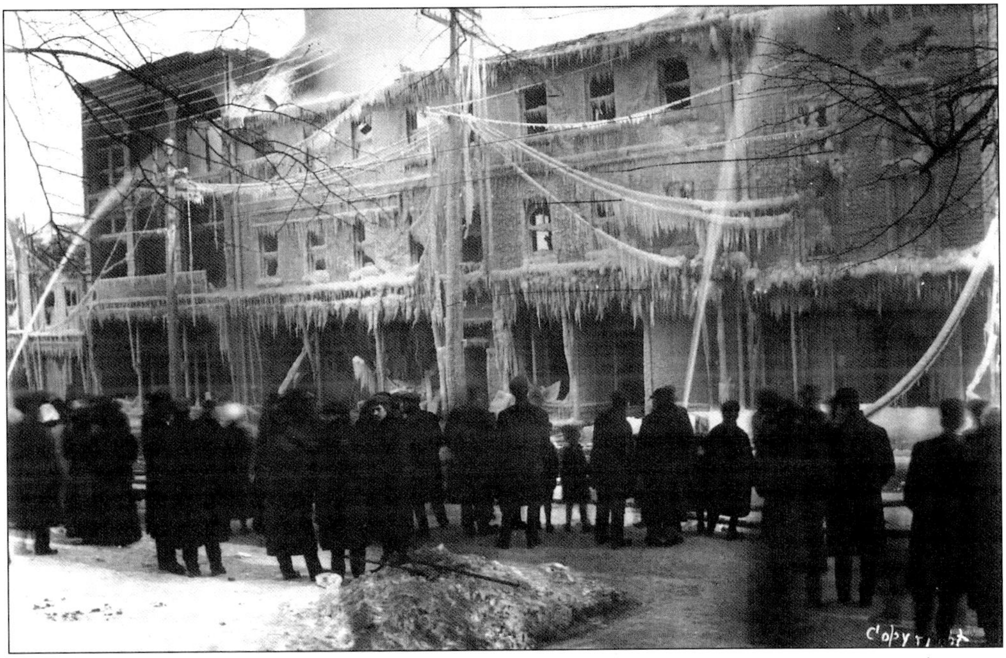

Pictured above are firemen fighting the Cragg Building fire on Barrington Street on the very same night. The Barnstead and Sutherland Buildings were also gutted. Due to the extremely cold weather, the water froze leaving an eerie sight at the scene of the blaze. The Cragg Bros. Hardware store opened in 1889, however the fire did not put them out of business, the depression of the 1930s did. (Courtesy of the Photograph Collection, Public Archives of Nova Scotia, Notman Collection, #20586.)

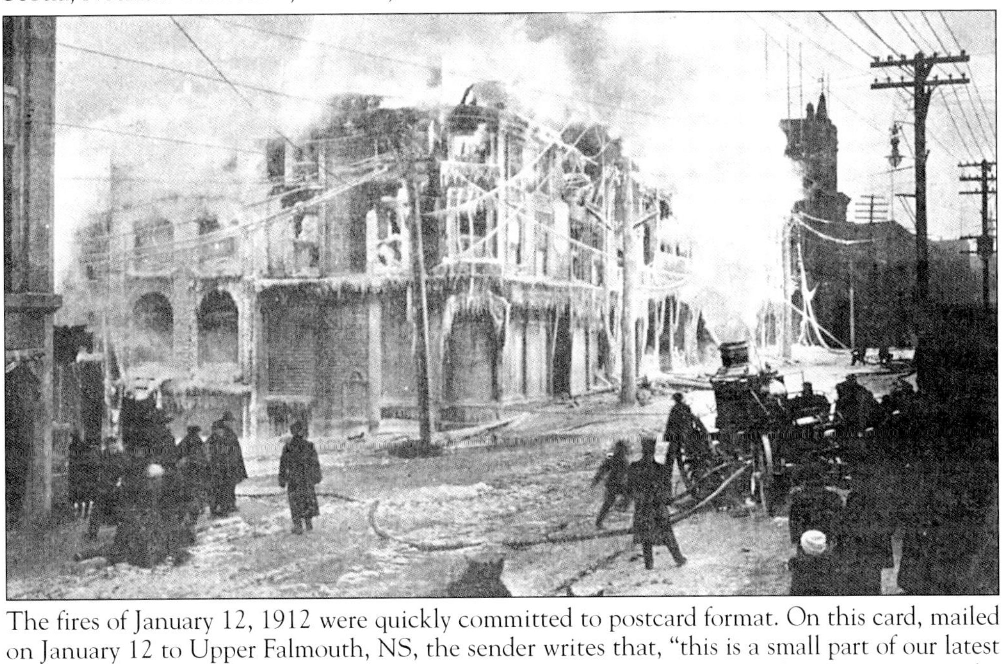

The fires of January 12, 1912 were quickly committed to postcard format. On this card, mailed on January 12 to Upper Falmouth, NS, the sender writes that, "this is a small part of our latest fire, they say Halifax is to be all burnt in 1912." The words became prophetic in a way as the Explosion did achieve the same in 1917.

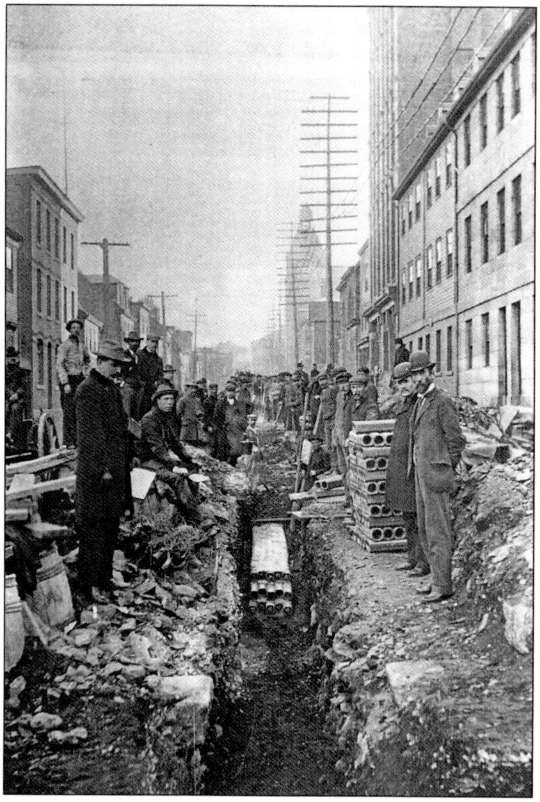

One of the technological advances of the late 19th century was the laying of underground cables in large cities. Here a large work force digs up Granville Street (facing south from Sackville Street) to lay cables as traffic squeezes by on the left of the picture. (Courtesy of the Photograph Collection, Public Archives of Nova Scotia, Marconi to the Satellite fonds, #74.)

One of the most attended funeral processions in the city was in 1875, for the oarsman, George Brown, who died July 8 of that year at only 36. The procession is seen below winding its way slowly down Barrington Street, with Nicholas Power and Garret Cotter in the buggy, four policemen at front, with Roger O'Brien, captain of the Engine Company on horseback. Members of the Halifax Rowing Club and the Paris Crew from St. John, NB acted as pallbearers. (Courtesy of the Photograph Collection, Public Archives of Nova Scotia, Tom Connors Old Sport, #211.)

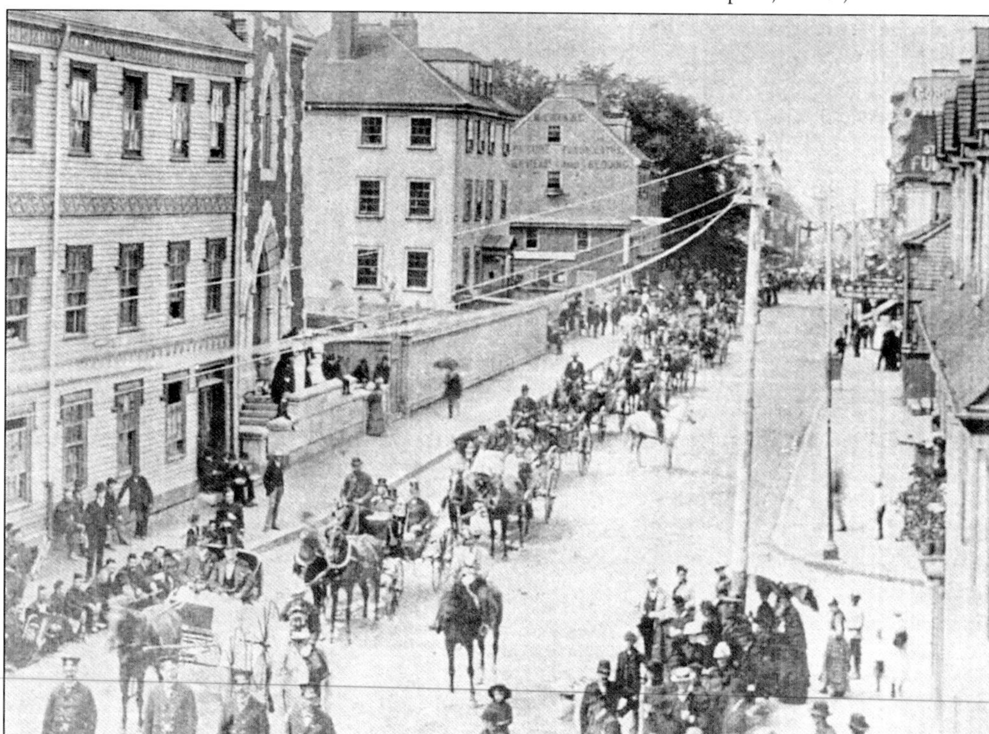

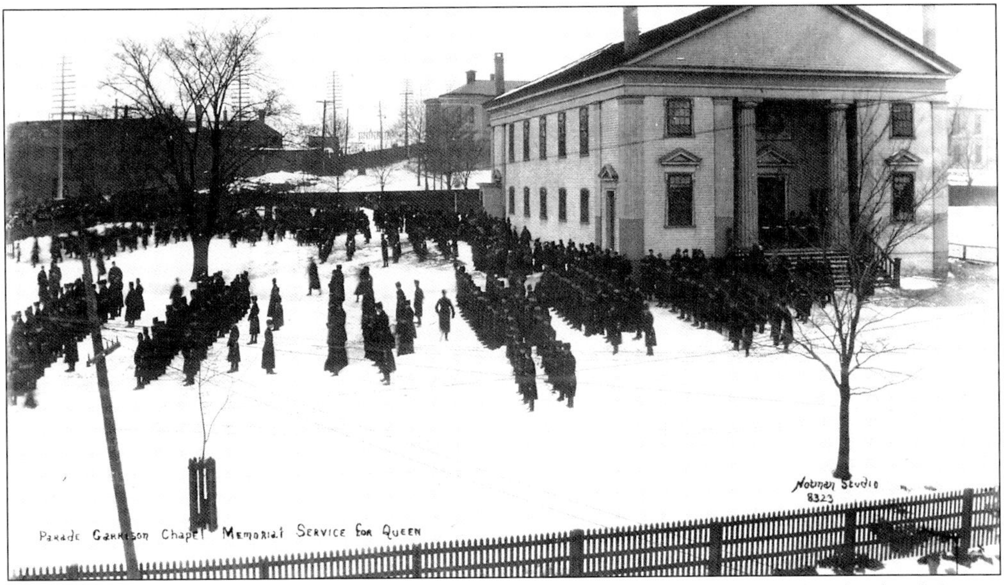

Here is a parade at the Garrison Chapel at a memorial service following the death of Queen Victoria in 1901. After 64 years as monarch (she is still the longest serving monarch in British history), the entire Empire was stunned by her passing. Many had only known Victoria as Queen in their lifetime, and the new century had started on a sad note. Even today, ironically, Victoria Day (May 18) is celebrated as a holiday in Canada, yet is not in Britain. (Courtesy of the Photograph Collection, Public Archives of Nova Scotia, Notman Collection, #8323.)

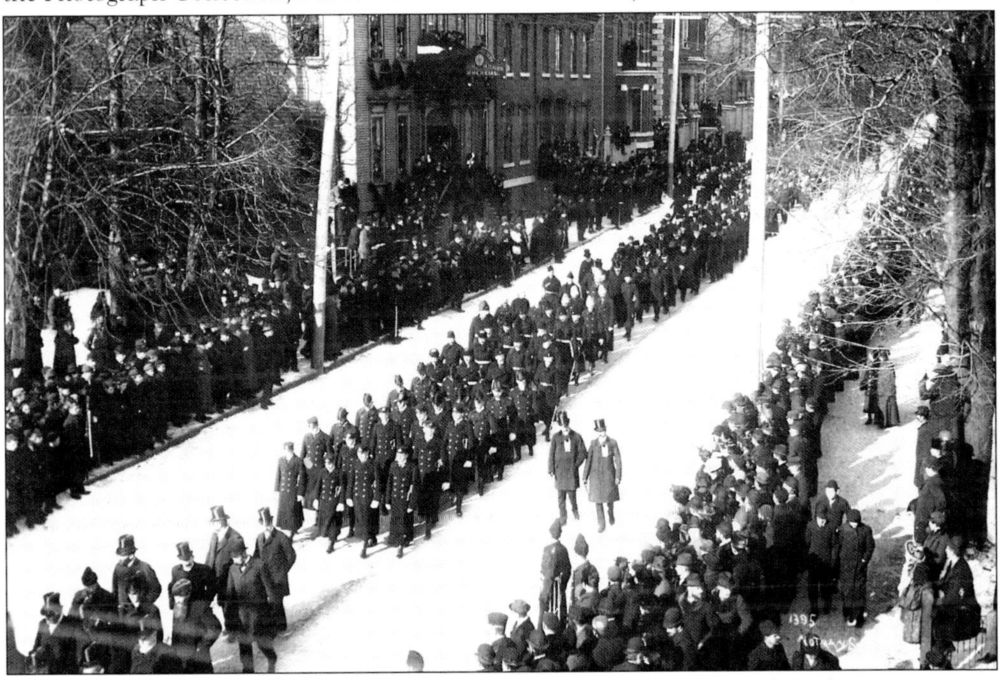

The final sombre picture shows the State Funeral procession of Sir John Thompson, prime minister of Canada, heading along Barrington Street on January 3, 1895. The Halifax Commercial Academy is the building in the centre of the photograph. (Courtesy of the Photograph Collection, Public Archives of Nova Scotia, Notman Collection, #1395.)

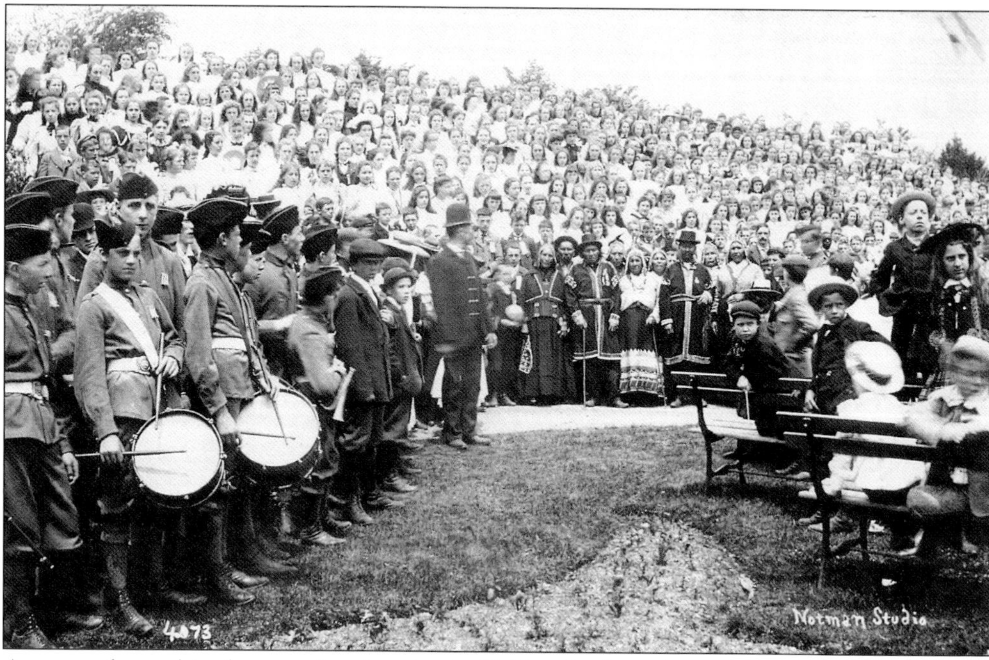

Among others, this photograph taken in the Public Gardens shows a mass of school children at the unveiling of the fountain in the park during Jubilee Week (celebrating the Queen's 60th year on the throne) in 1897. (Courtesy of the Photograph Collection, Public Archives of Nova Scotia, Notman Collection, #4073.)

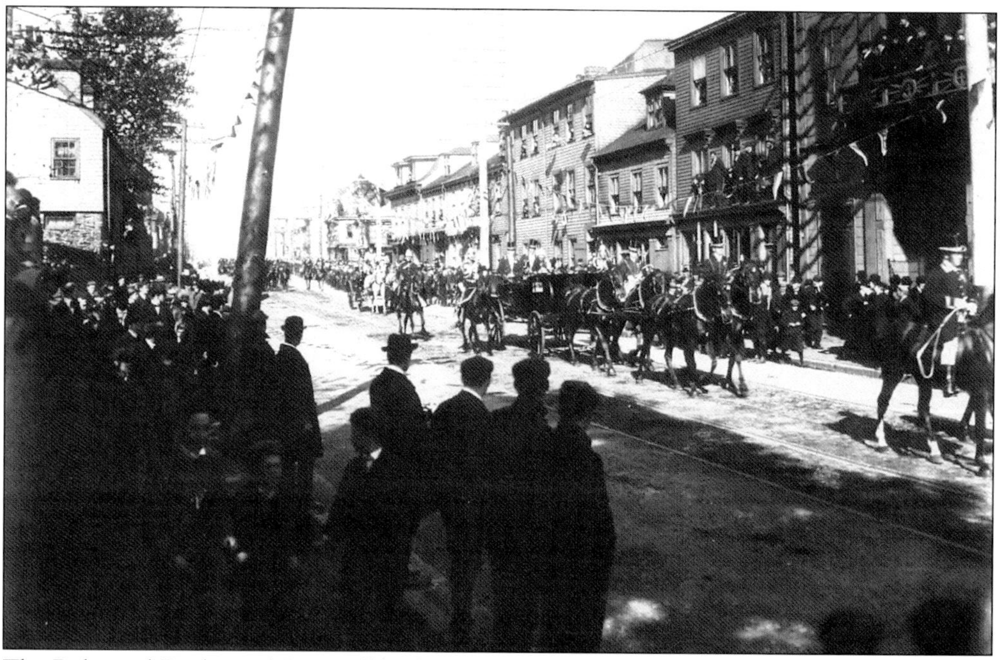

The Duke and Duchess of Cornwall and York paid a visit to Halifax in October of 1901. They later became King George V and Queen Mary after the death of Edward VII in 1910. The procession passes between the streetcar tracks on Barrington Street. (Courtesy of the Photograph Collection, Public Archives of Nova Scotia, W. L. Bishop collection, #76.)

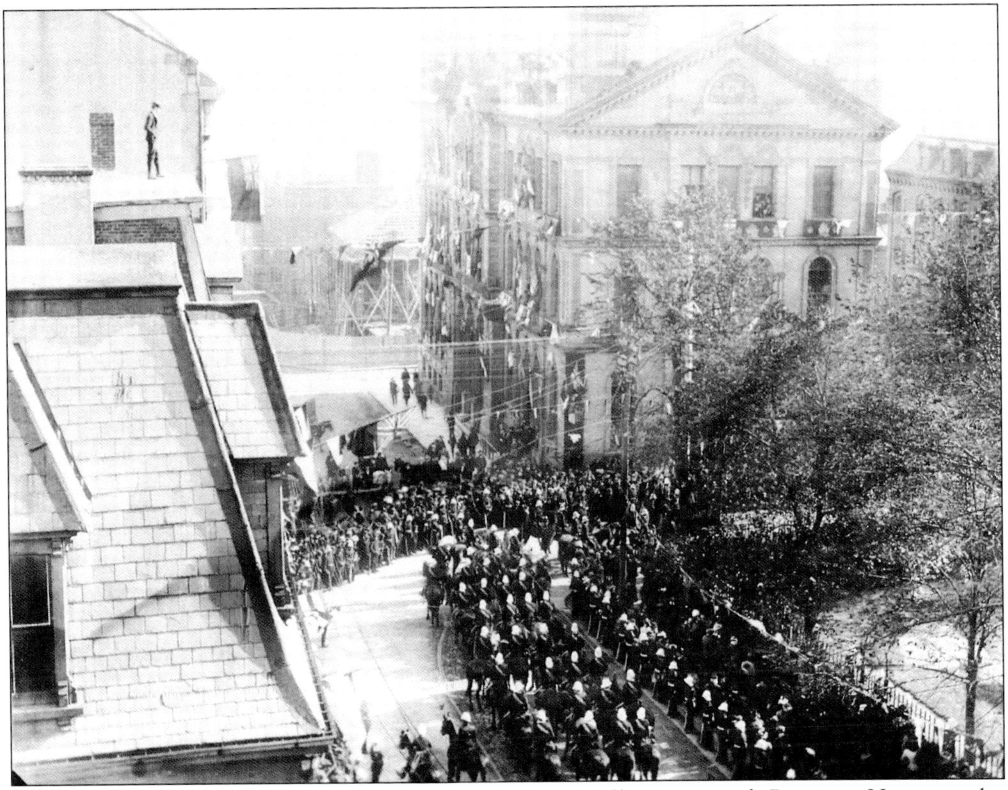

The Royal Tour of the Duke and Duchess heads along Hollis Street with Province House on the right. The large building in the centre of the picture is the post office; the building having its roof repaired behind it is the Market building, erected in 1851. The Merchant's Bank building, built in 1877 to 1878, provides an excellent yet precarious vantage point for one spectator. (Courtesy of the Photograph Collection, Public Archives of Nova Scotia, Halifax: Special Events 54.1.)

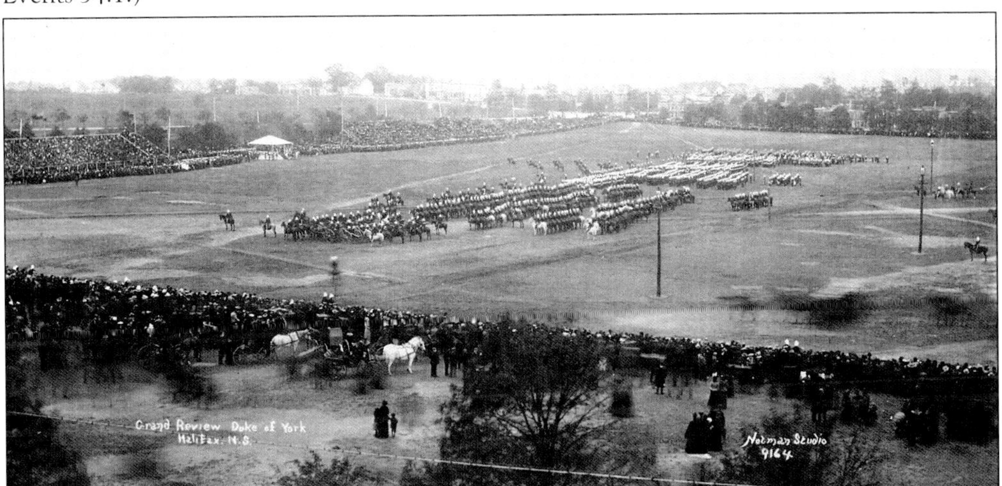

This spectacular panorama shows the Grand Review with the Duke of York, on the Royal Visit of 1901. The picture was taken on the commons. (Courtesy of the Photograph Collection, Public Archives of Nova Scotia, Notman Collection, #9164.)

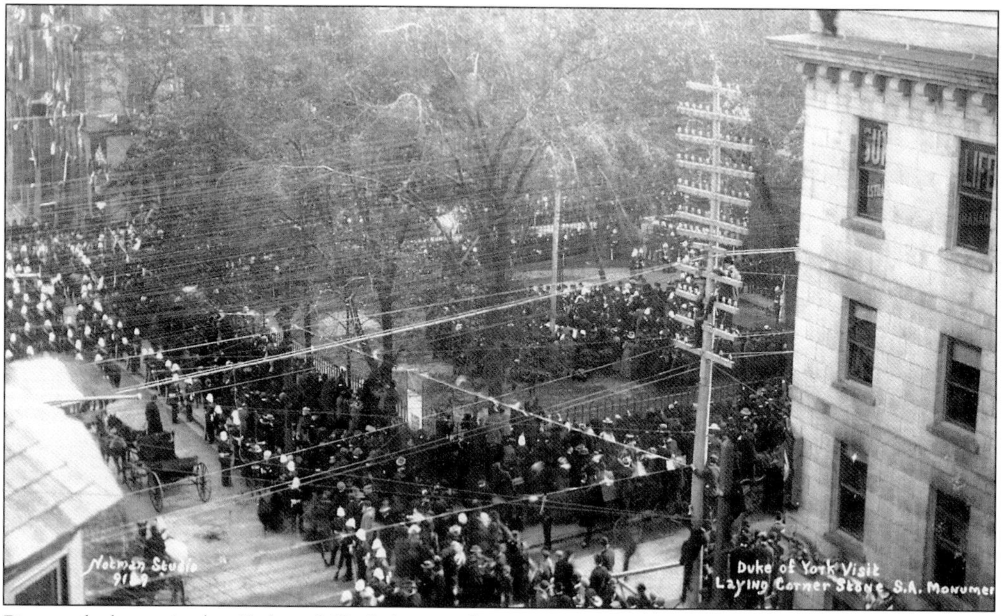

Pictured above is the Duke of York laying the cornerstone of the South African Monument at Province House in 1901. The photograph appears foggy toward the top, until it is realized the cause is the phenomenal number of wires being carried along the street. And how the gentlemen managed to scale that very pole for a perfect view is also open to question! (Courtesy of the Photograph Collection, Public Archives of Nova Scotia, Notman Collection, #9189.)

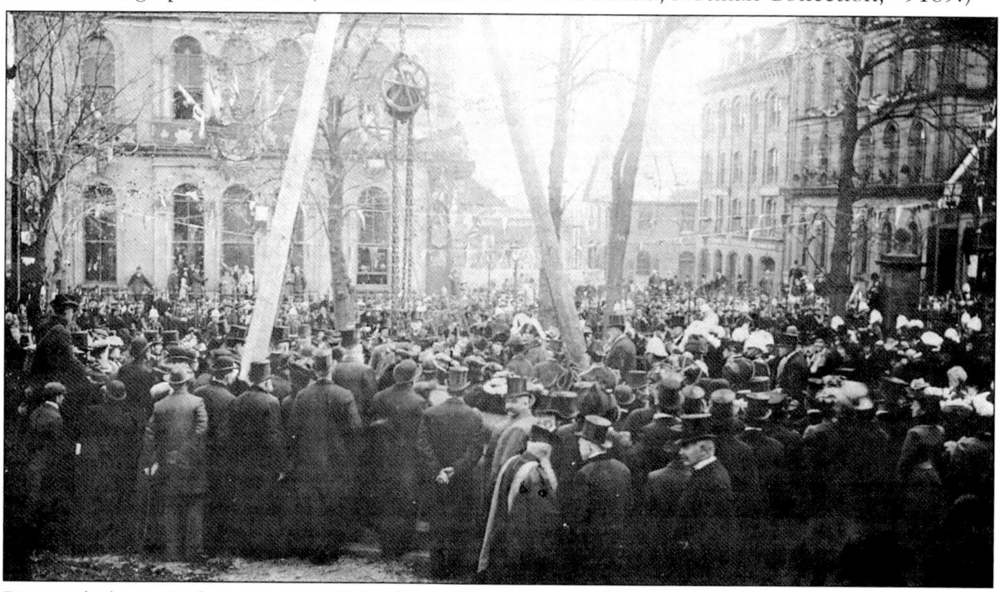

Pictured above is the erection of the Boer War Memorial (South African Monument) on the North Side of Province House in 1901. Canada sent 14,000 horses and 6,000 troops to the Boer War. The regiments were the Canadian Scouts, the Royal Canadian Dragons, the Royal Canadian Regiment of Infantry, the Royal Canadian Mounted Rifles, the Second Regiment of the Canadian Mounted Rifles, and Lord Strathcona's Corps. (Courtesy of the Photograph Collection, Public Archives of Nova Scotia, Halifax: Miscellaneous: Memorial: Boer War 54.3.)

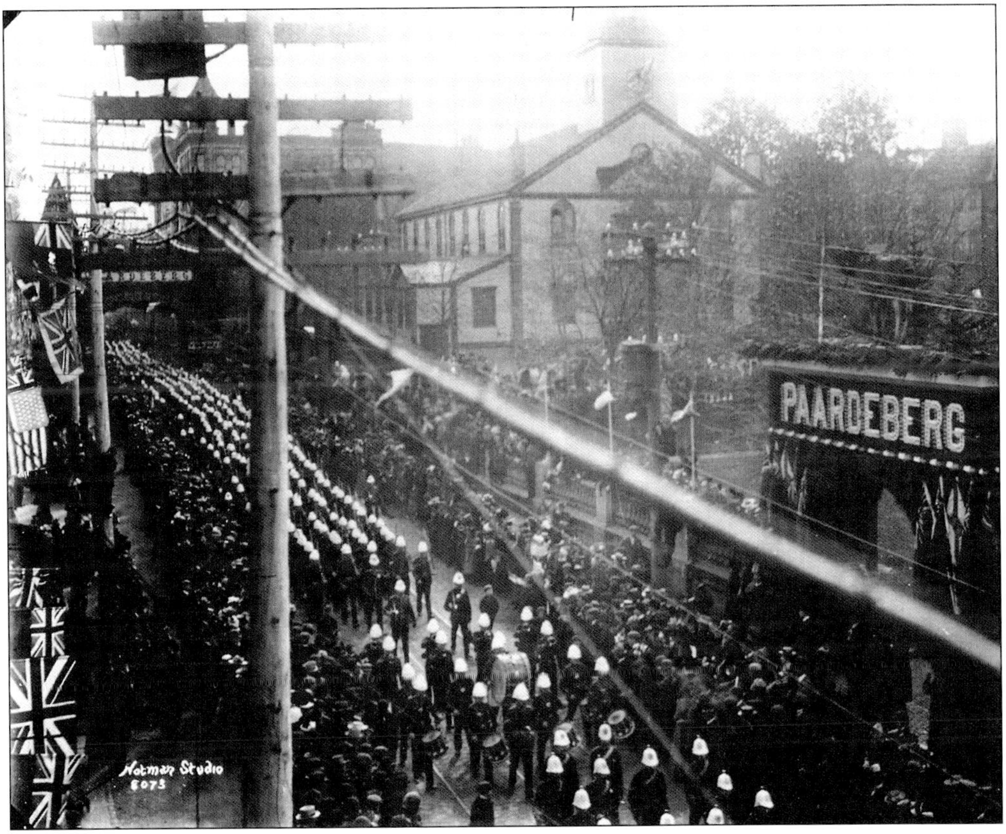

The Boer War was officially over in 1902, and Barrington Street, used to the occasional parade, was again the venue for this picture of the returning troops victory parade. St. Paul's Church is clearly visible, as is a decorated arch celebrating the Canadian forces' involvement in the battle of Paardeberg on February 18, 1900. (Courtesy of the Photograph Collection, Public Archives of Nova Scotia, Notman Collection #8073.)

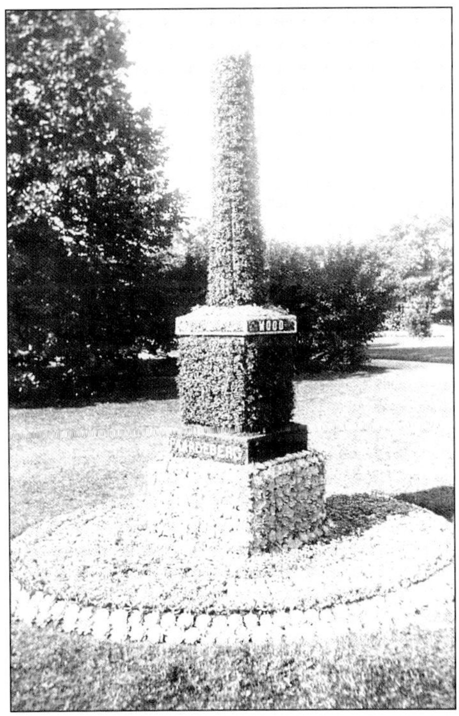

This monument to the Boer War and the battle at Paardeberg was made entirely from shrubbery at the Public Gardens. Close to two hundred Canadians died during the war, almost a half of them due to illness, including dysentery, sunstroke, and tonsillitis. Of the 22,000 British troops who lost their lives, almost 13,000 were due to disease. (Courtesy of the Photograph Collection, Public Archives of Nova Scotia, J.A. Irvine Collection, Album #36, #94.)

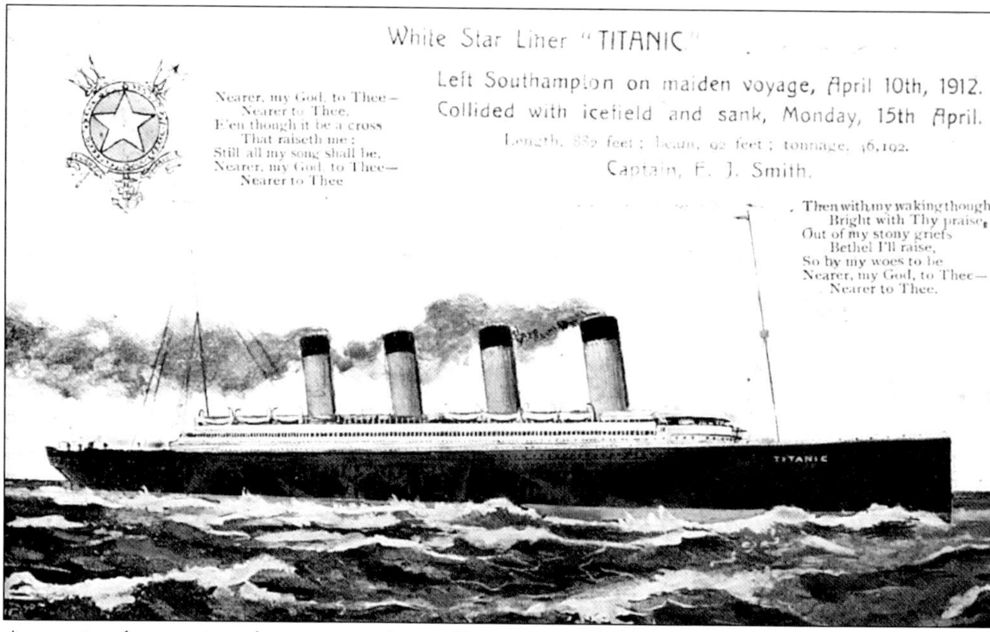

As previously mentioned, one event that will seemingly always be connected with several places is the Titanic Disaster of April 15, 1912. Those places include Southampton, its departure point, and New York, its destination, along with Newfoundland, its closest point at sinking, and Halifax, where many of the bodies and survivors were taken. This April 1912 postcard was sold in aid of the Titanic Disaster Fund, and advertises on its reverse a Disaster Fund service for April 28, along with a list of music to be played.

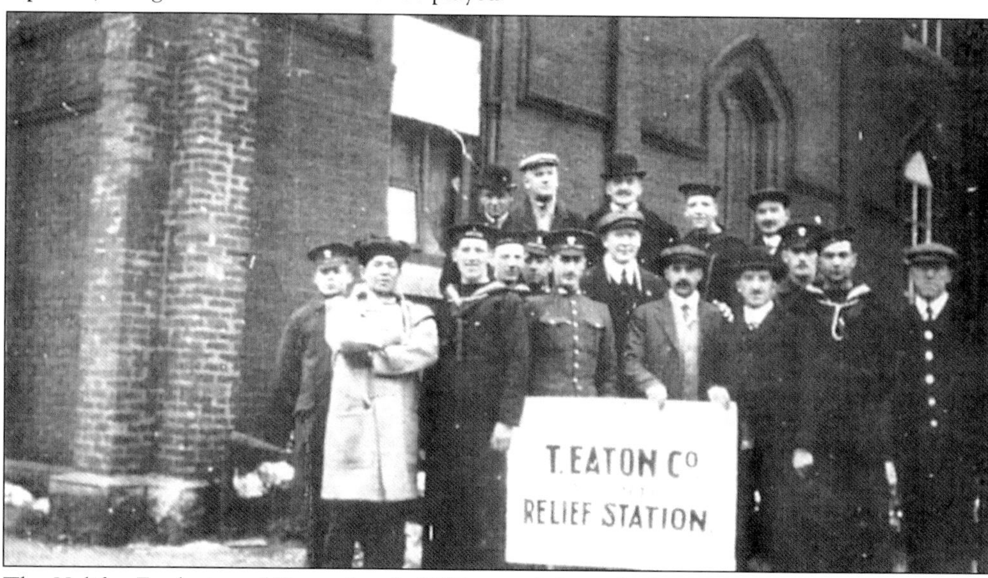

The Halifax Explosion of December 6, 1917 ripped through the city, causing appalling loss of life. Over two thousand died in the Explosion. Relief began to pour in from all four corners of the globe. New England was especially kind, an act which has not been forgotten as Halifax each year sends a Christmas tree to the city of Boston. This picture shows the Relief Station of Eaton's at the Hall of the First Baptist Church on Queen Street. (Courtesy of the Photograph Collection, Public Archives of Nova Scotia, Mary P. Freeman Collection, #17.)

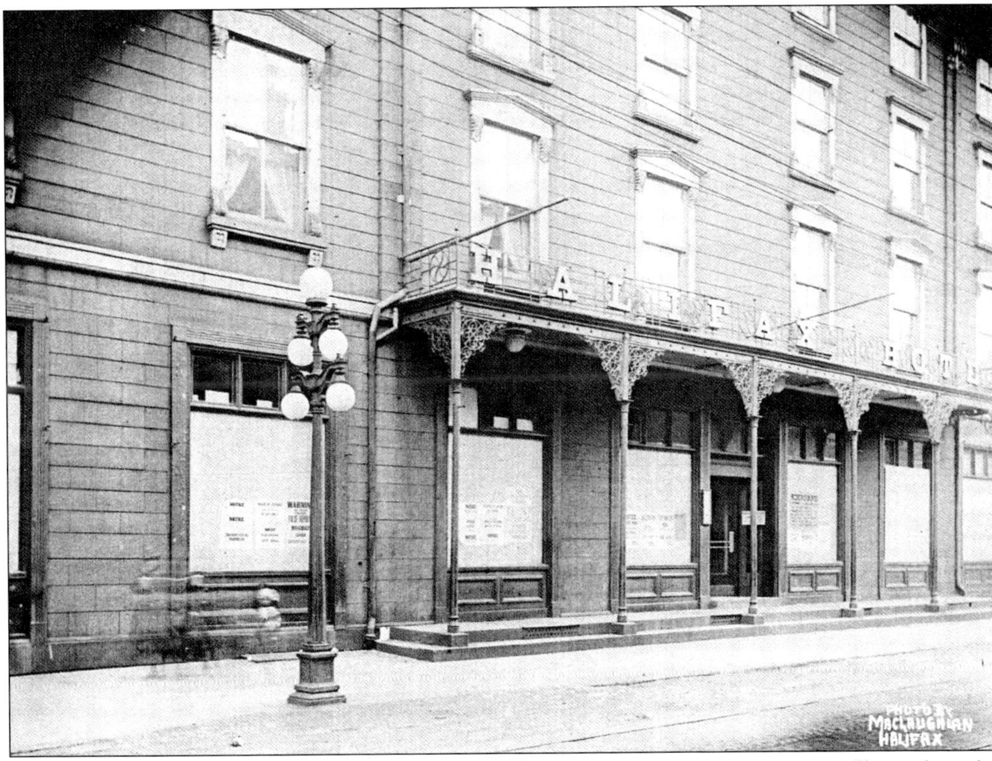

The Halifax Hotel on Hollis Street became the temporary reconstruction office after the Explosion. The night after the disaster, there was a huge snowstorm, which hampered efforts further. Each year, at 9 a.m. on December 6, the exact time of the Explosion, a service is held to remember one of the most painful moments in Halifax's long history. (Courtesy of the Photograph Collection, Public Archives of Nova Scotia, Halifax: Explosion 53.2.)

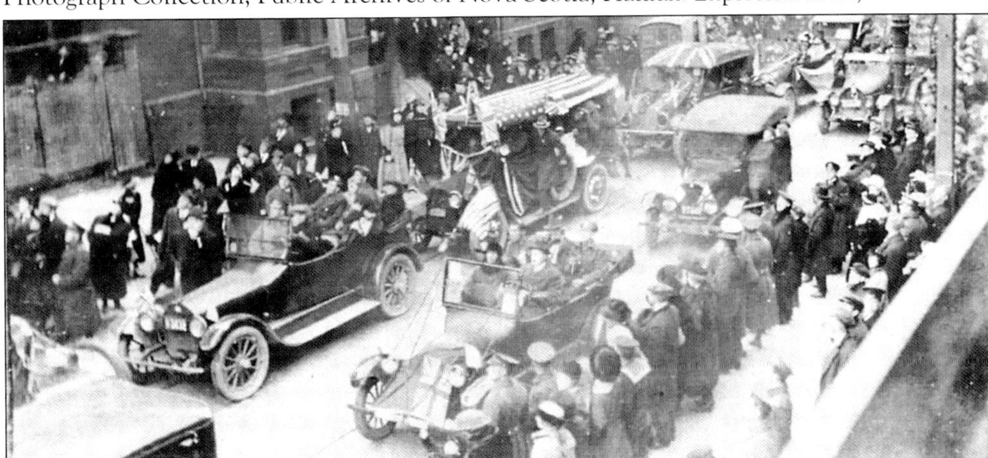

If it's a parade it must be Barrington Street, and this picture of the Armistice Day Parade is no exception. The parade went around much of the city, Spring Garden Road and South Park Street, and understandably the mood was one of unbridled jubilation with Union Flags everywhere, along with the occasional Stars and Stripes for good measure. (Courtesy of the Photograph Collection, Public Archives of Nova Scotia, Halifax: Special Events: Armistice Day 54.1.)

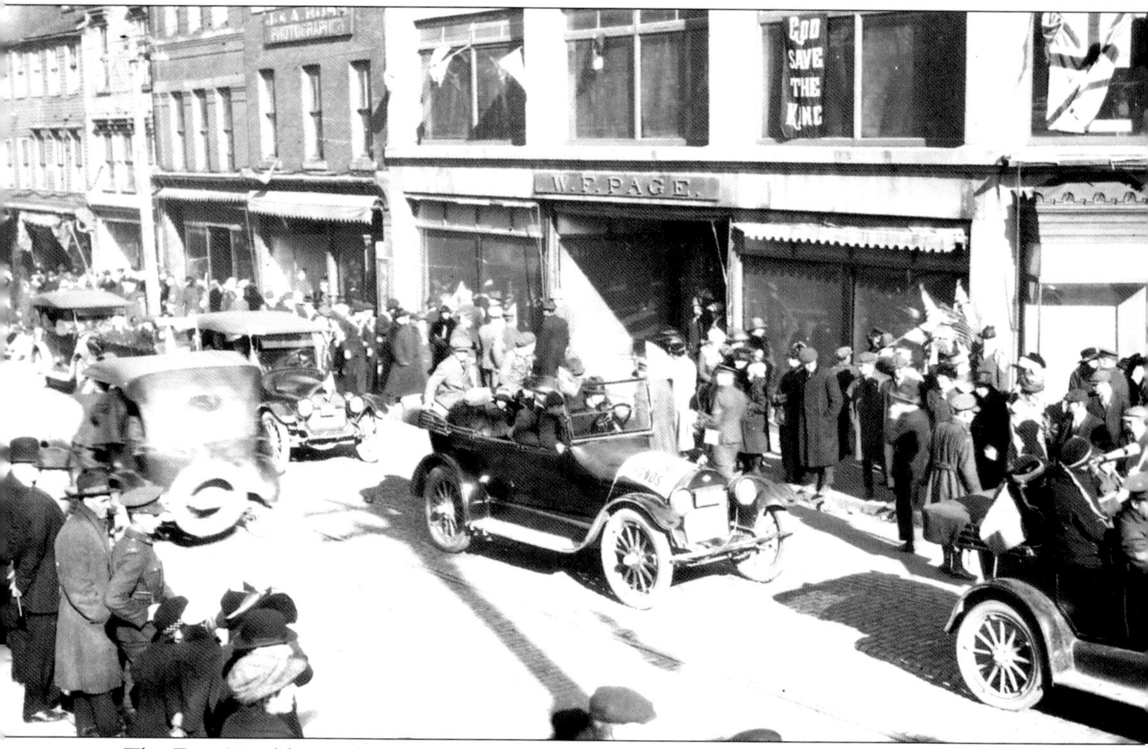

The First World War finally ended on November 11, 1918. According to the *Halifax Herald* of the following day, sirens blew, bells rang, flags flew out of windows, and cars were all over the streets. A whole page advertisement in the newspaper declared "Peace," and November 12 was declared a civic holiday. With hindsight, the peace slogans appear very sad, as 21 years later, the Second World War broke out. Fathers who had been to war watched in horror as their sons did the same. The "War to end all Wars," unfortunately did not. The joy of this parade winding past the W.F. Page store and Ross, Photographers at least signaled the happy end of the Great War. An advertisement on one of the vehicles urges the purchase of "Victory Bonds." (Courtesy of the Photograph Collection, Public Archives of Nova Scotia, Arthur Bloomfield Dawson fonds, series 1, #216.)

Nine

Recreation

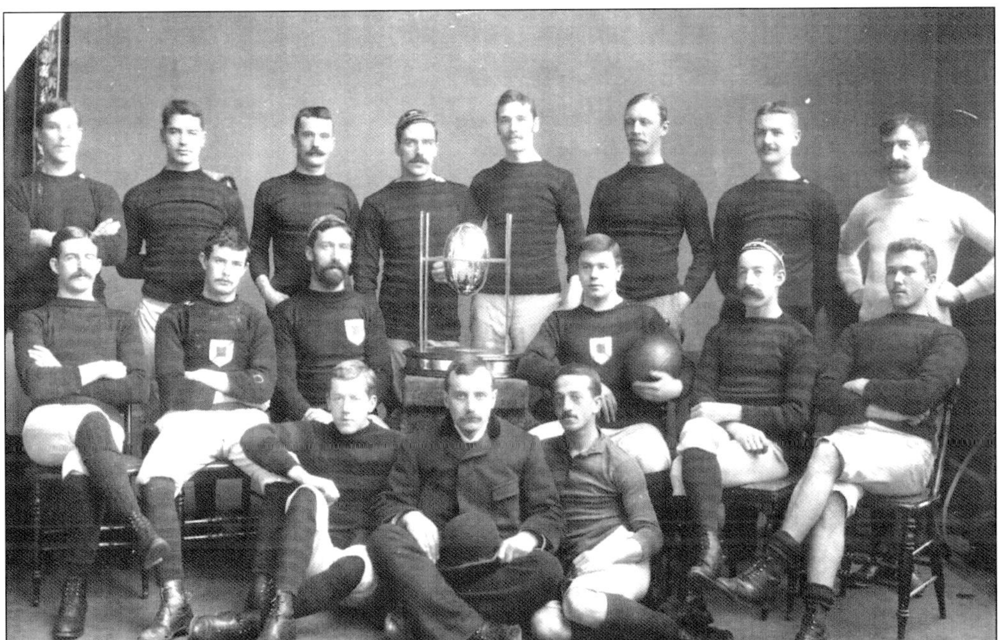

This was the Wanderers football group with their trophy, c. 1892. (Courtesy of the Photograph Collection, Public Archives of Nova Scotia, Notman Collection, #71901.)

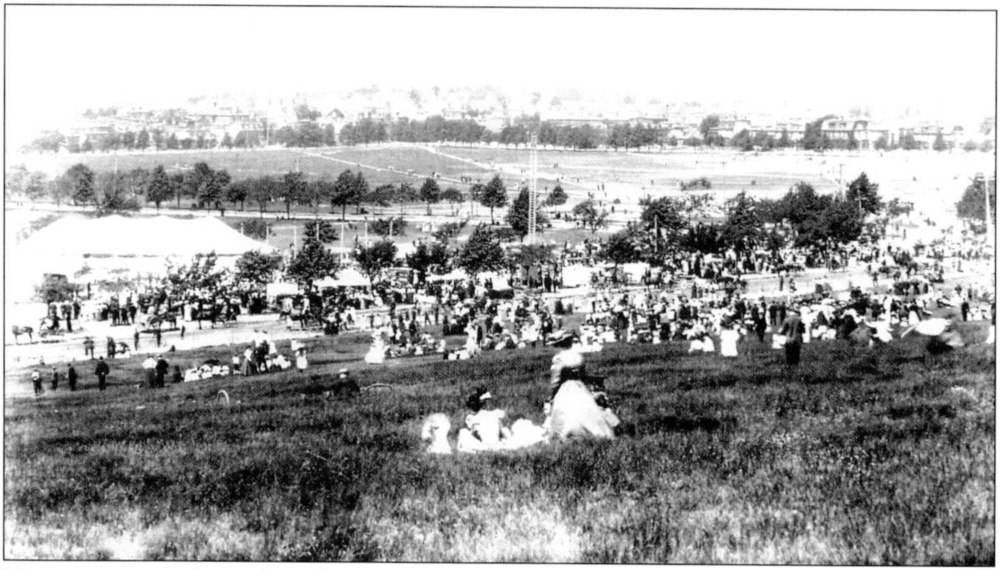

Many circuses and traveling shows came to Halifax in the late 1800s and at the turn of the century. This c. 1900 photograph shows the tent and in the centre of the picture, a ladder with a high-diving act. The show took place on the north commons and is seen here from Citadel Hill. (Courtesy of the Photograph Collection, Public Archives of Nova Scotia, W.L. Bishop Collection #60.)

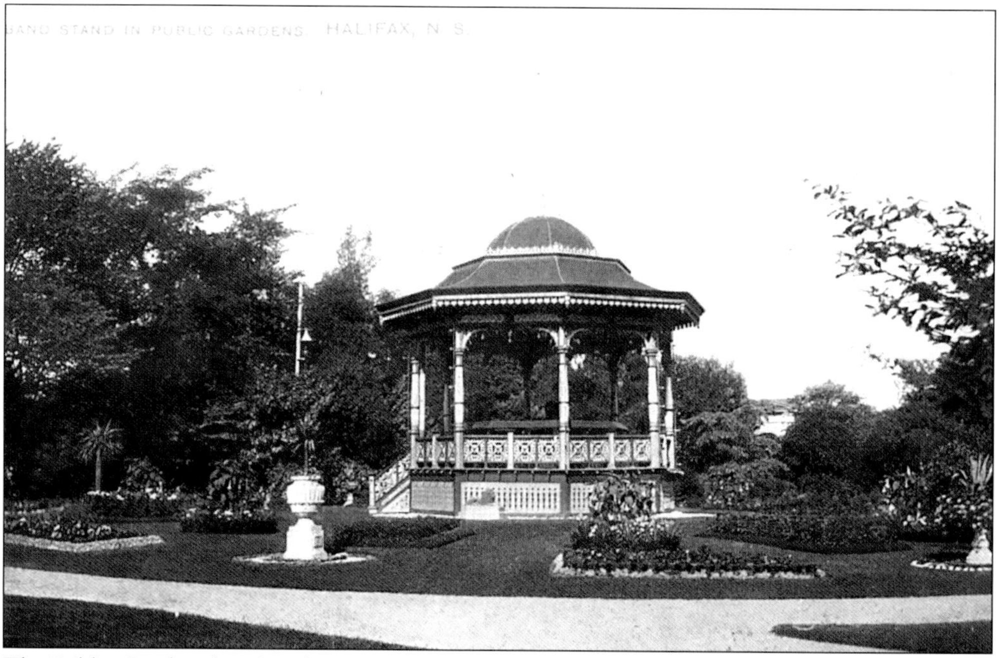

The Public Gardens has for a long time provided a haven in Halifax for music and strolling. The bandstand seen here was erected in 1887. The park is enclosed by a wrought iron fence with ornamental gates made in Glasgow, Scotland in 1889. Responsibility for the original garden (run by the Nova Scotia Horticultural Society in 1836) and a civic garden (1867) passed to the City of Halifax in 1874.

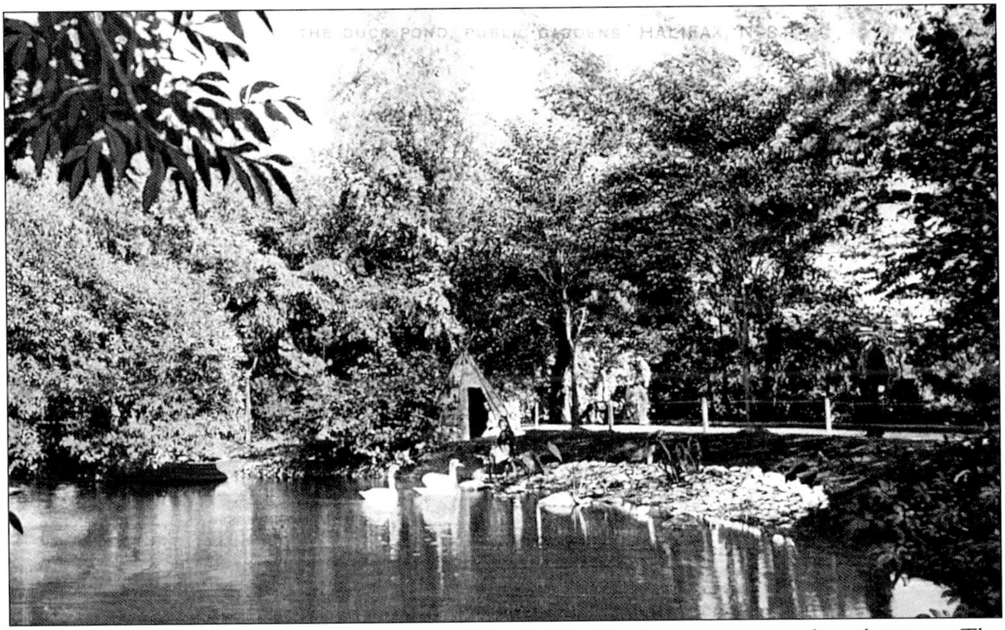

The Duck Pond has always been a feature of the Public Gardens to attract a lot of visitors. The garden itself began as a private garden in 1753. The present design, by Richard Power, who was gardener to the Duke of Devonshire in Ireland, was finalized in 1875.

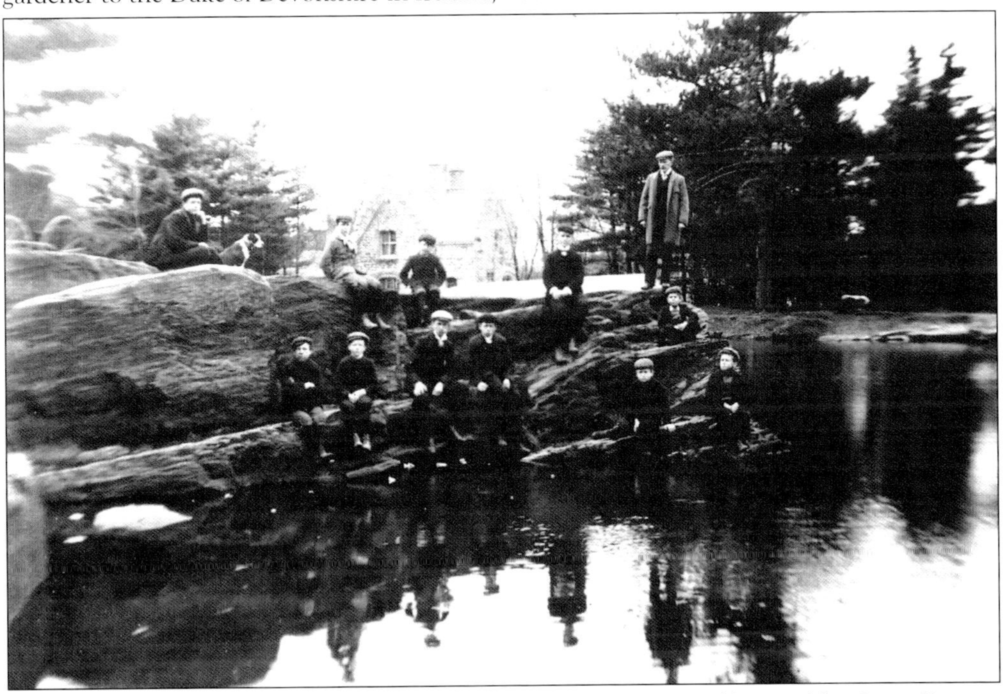

Point Pleasant Park, the 186-acre site at the south of Halifax is still owned by Great Britain, and is leased at the very reasonable sum of one shilling per year. This photograph shows a group of boys sitting at the Quarry Pond, with the Gatekeeper's Lodge in the background. (Courtesy of the Photograph Collection, Public Archives of Nova Scotia, J.A. Irvine Collection, Album #36, #36.)

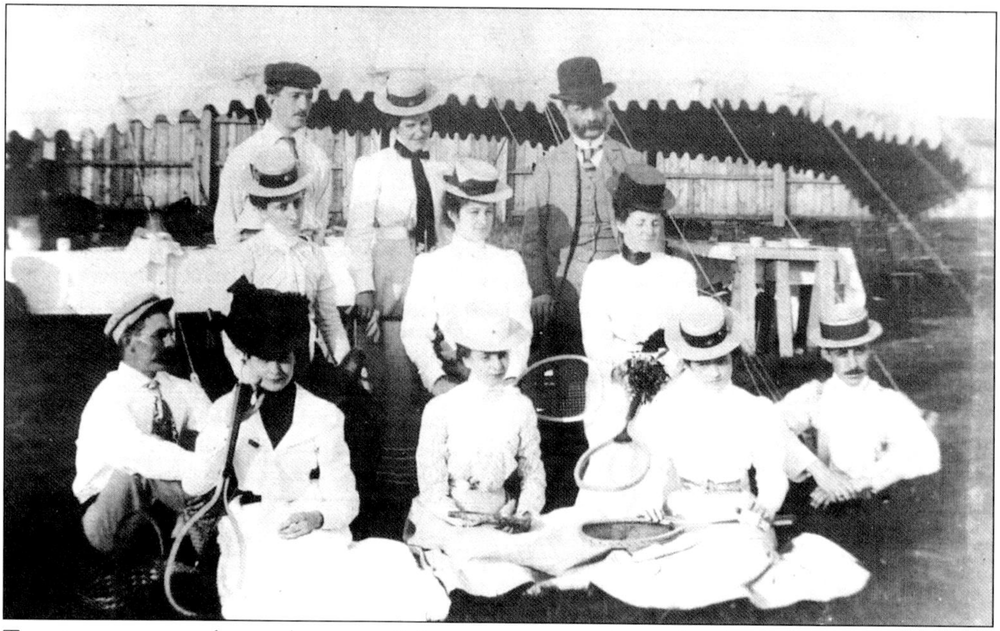

Tennis was as popular at the turn of the century as it always has been. Ironically with the evolution of the tennis racquet, the metal frames of today look remarkably similar to these wooden ones. These pictures were taken at the polo fields. Tennis began on the Public Gardens in 1876. The South End Tennis Club was established by Mr. G. McG. Mitchell in 1890. (Courtesy of the Photograph Collection, Public Archives of Nova Scotia, J.A. Irvine Collection, Album #36, #75.)

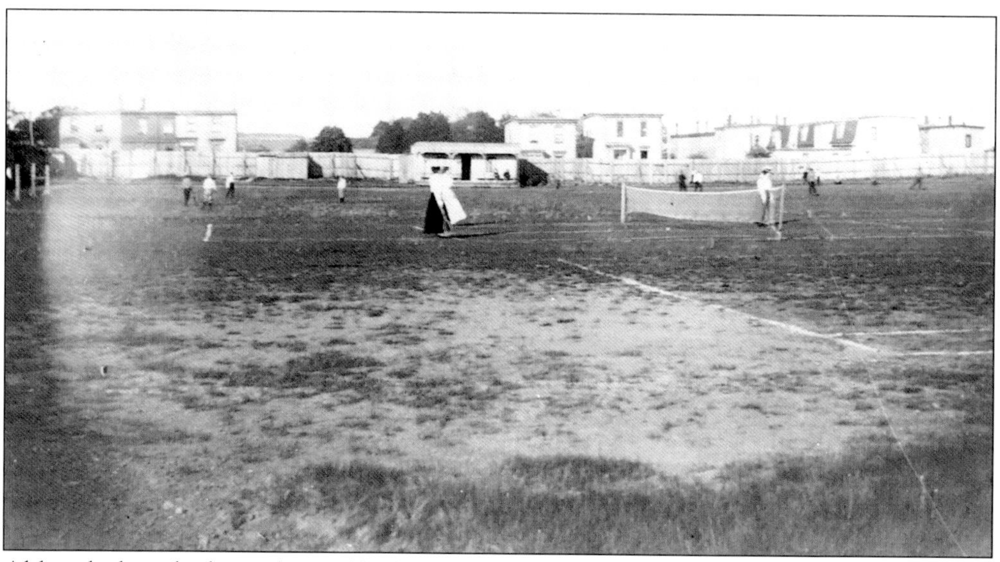

Although the rules have changed little, there were those who found the game distasteful. *The Critic* newspaper of June 19, 1891, in an editorial, berated tennis with respect to archery—"we often wonder why the graceful and healthful sport of archery has become so altogether forgotten. It gives an even better opportunity than tennis for the display of personal charms, and this is not to be disregarded." Pete Sampras, beware. (Courtesy of the Photograph Collection, Public Archives of Nova Scotia, J.A. Irvine Collection, Album #36, #87.)

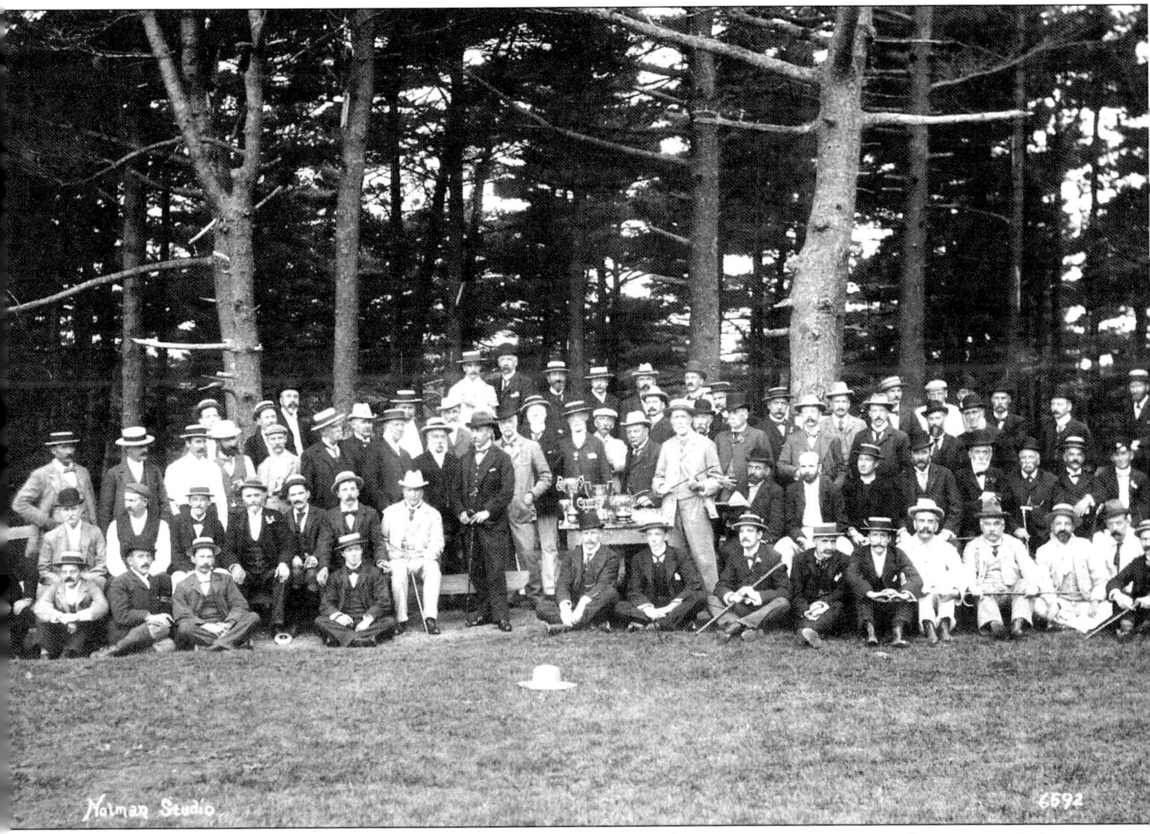

Speaking of sports which have died out, quoits, one of the major sports at the turn of the century, is now almost forgotten, although some remnants of the game still exist in the city today. This photograph shows the assembled Studley Quoit Club taken on August 26, 1899. Not just a sporting club, the Studley Club was also a social event, and many of the city notables took it upon themselves to join. The picture also shows the male domination of the game. Other summer sports included baseball, first played in Dartmouth in 1841, golf, tennis, and cricket. (Courtesy of the Photograph Collection, Public Archives of Nova Scotia, Notman Collection, #6592.)

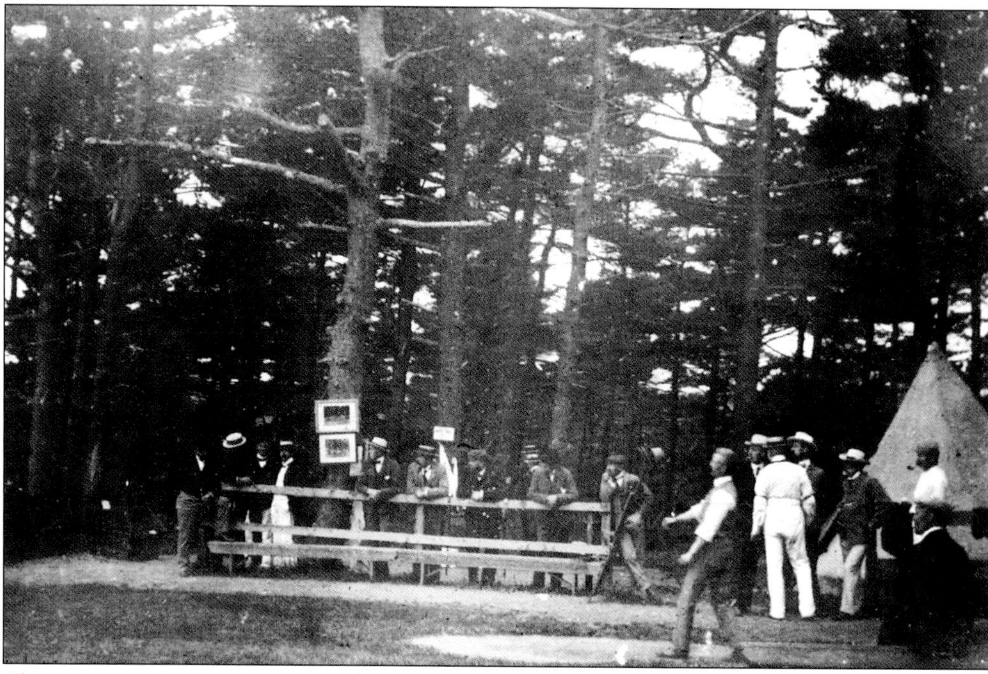

There are very few photographs of quoits actually being played. This picture, from a collection of the Studley Quoit Club, shows the 'action.' The 30-acre Studley Estate, owned by Judge (later Sir Alexander) Croke, was named after his English home, and was later purchased by Dalhousie University, although quoits were still played by the Club at the corner of Oxford and South Streets. The Studley Quoit Club was formed in 1858 with 14 members. (Courtesy of the Photograph Collection, Public Archives of Nova Scotia, Studley Quoit Club Collection, #48.)

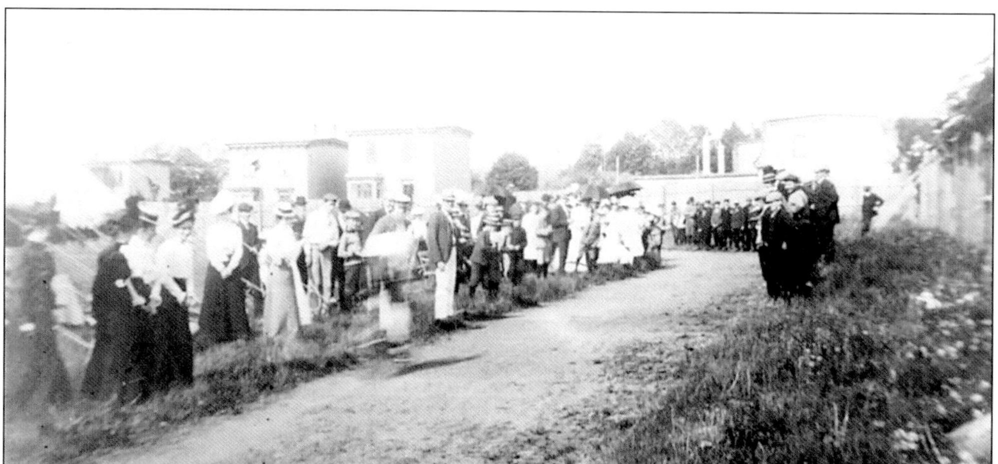

Here is a foot race taking place at the polo field. The spectators are clearly visible, however, due to the exposure time of the camera, the runners are a mere blur toward the left of the picture. In the *Halifax Herald* of December 13, 1909, an article in the sports section quoted Dr. Watson L. Savage, physical director of Pittsburg Athletic Association and formerly of Columbia University, as saying "ten miles is about the limit one should run." (Courtesy of the Photograph Collection, Public Archives of Nova Scotia, J.A. Irvine Collection, Album #36, #79.)

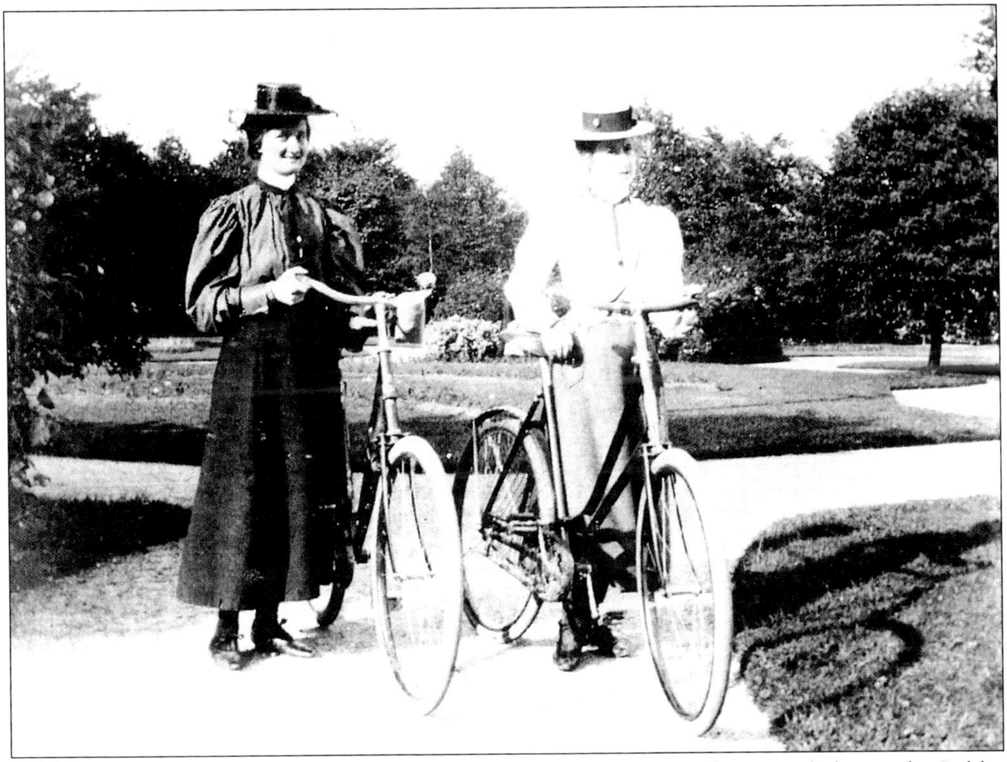

Cycling was also a great pastime around the turn of the century, as these two ladies in the Public Gardens show. Note the distinct lack of brakes. (Courtesy of the Photograph Collection, Public Archives of Nova Scotia, J.A. Irvine Collection, Album #37, #135.)

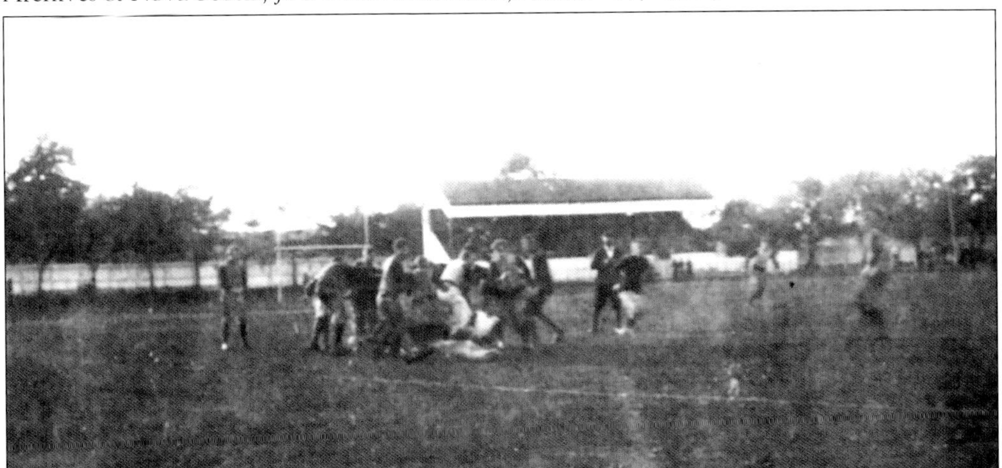

Another popular sport from Britain was rugby football, seen here being played on the Wanderers Ground. The Wanderers was a popular sporting name around the turn of the century, as it was the name of the top Association Football (soccer) team in England at that time. The Wanderers Amateur Athletic Association, which was involved in cricket, athletics, hockey, and football, was set up in 1882. The grounds opened in 1888, with a clubhouse added in 1896. (Courtesy of the Photograph Collection, Public Archives of Nova Scotia, J.A. Irvine Collection, Album #37, #136.)

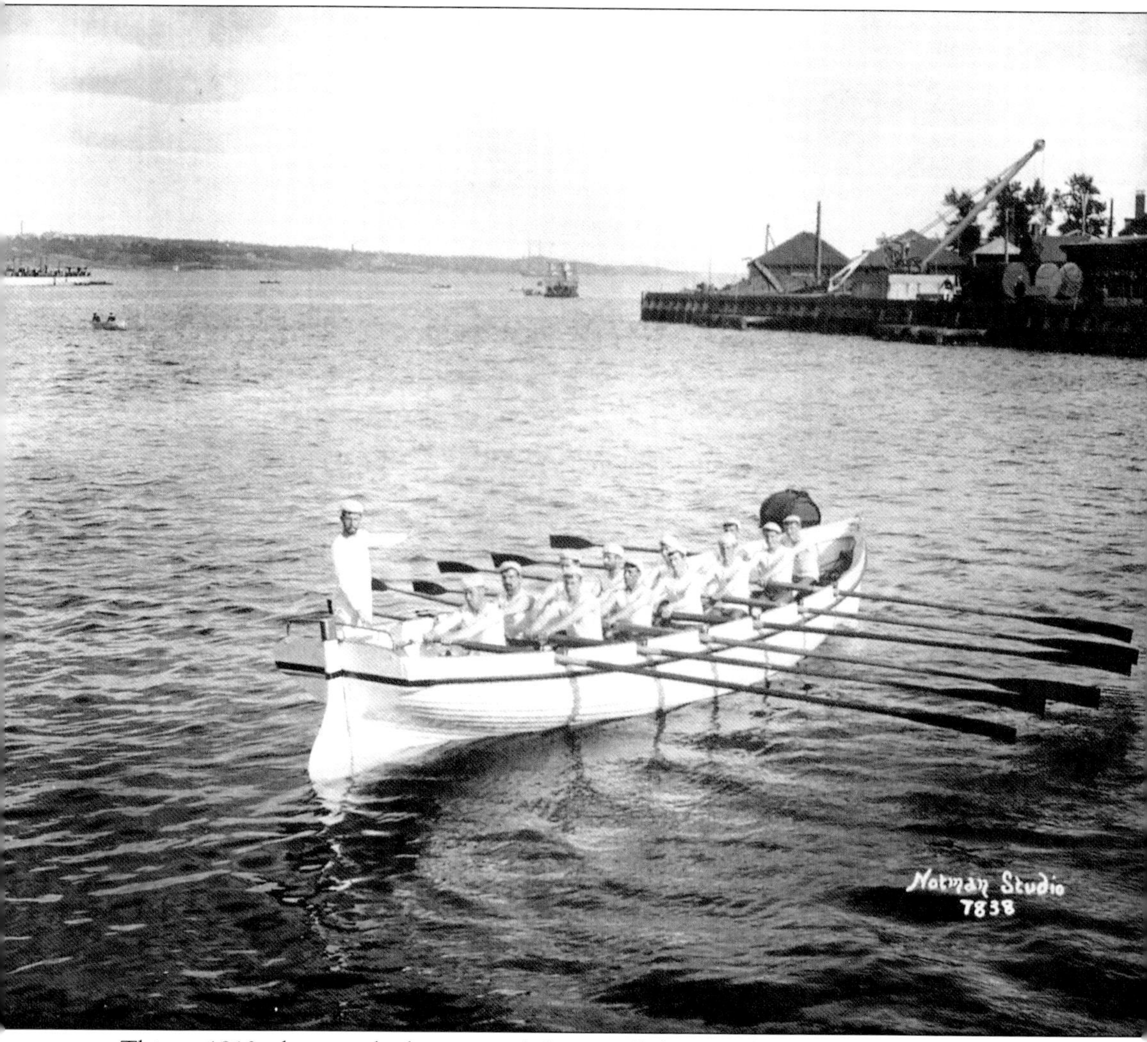

This c. 1910 photograph shows naval dories off the Royal Engineers Wharf. The 12-oared cutter is pictured here with its crew of 13. Thanks to its naval and sporting history, Halifax has always played an important part in sporting events involving water. Races involving many yacht clubs and rowing clubs took place in and around the city, including in the harbour, the Northwest Arm, and many of the lakes. In 1921, the famous Bluenose was built in Nova Scotia in Lunenburg, and shared its fame and heritage with Nova Scotia's capital of Halifax. (Courtesy of the Photograph Collection, Public Archives of Nova Scotia, Notman Collection, #7838.)

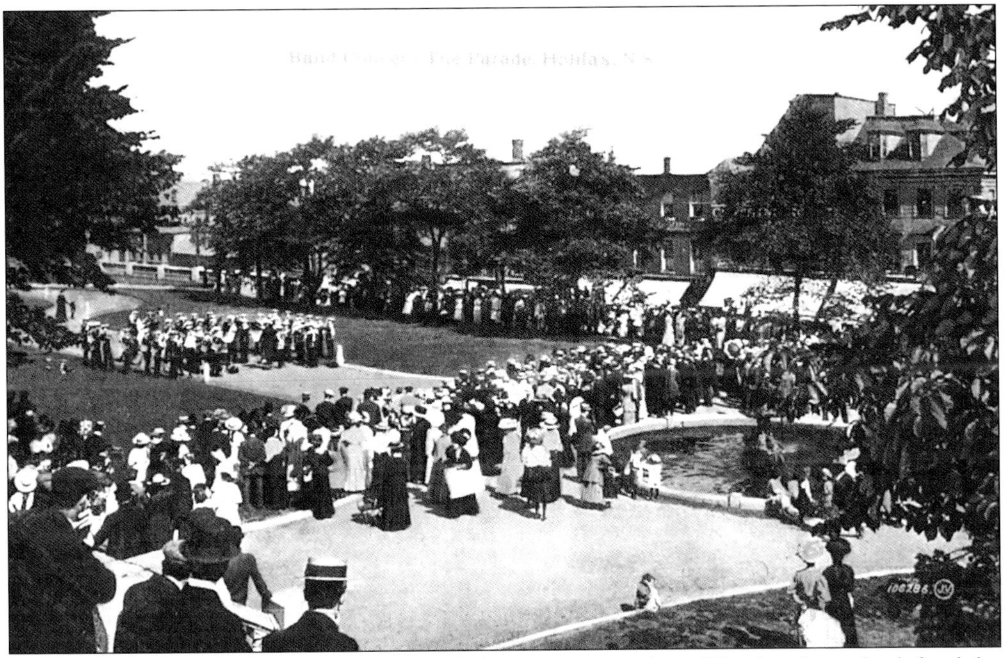

The only way to hear music at the turn of the century was live. The band, to the left of the picture, played a concert here at the Parade, one of several venues, including the Public Gardens, where outdoor concerts were regularly held.

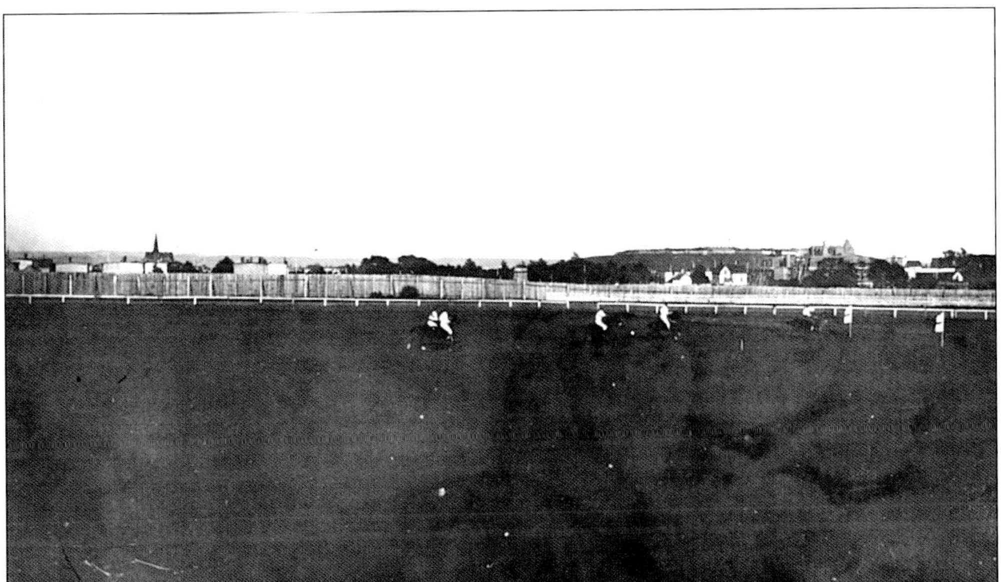

Another sport, or pastime, popular thanks to the British military influence, was the sport of polo. Several grounds existed, this one being the field surrounded by Quinpool Road, Oxford Street, and Chebucto Road. (Courtesy of the Photograph Collection, Public Archives of Nova Scotia, Halifax: Sports: Polo.)

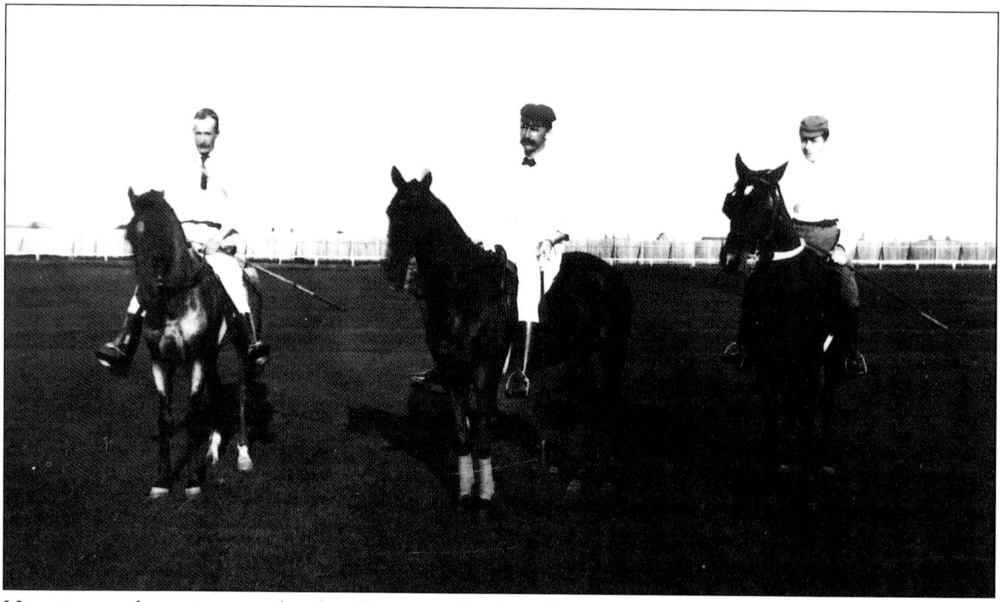

Here is another picture of polo players with their horses at the Polo Grounds *c.* 1889. The polo club was founded in 1878, and it is believed Halifax was the only venue for the sport in Canada. (Courtesy of the Photograph Collection, Public Archives of Nova Scotia, Halifax: Sports: Polo.)

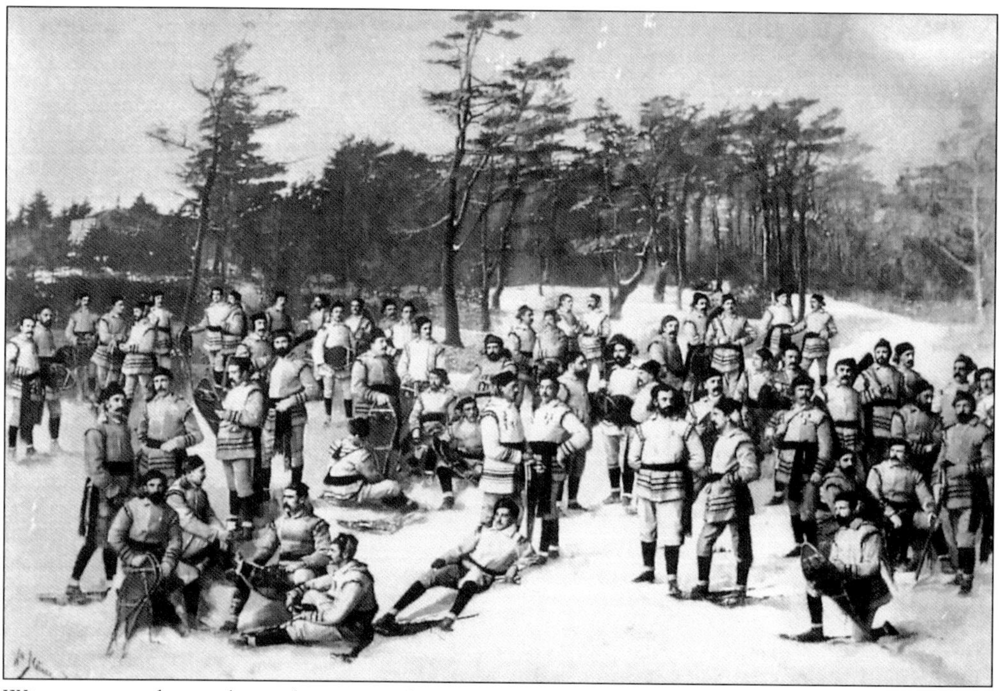

Winter sports have always been popular in Halifax. One long-lived sport was snowshoeing. The Red Cap Snowshoe Group is seen in this photograph, *c.* 1890. The Group was formed in December of 1874, and lasted for one hundred years before a difficulty in obtaining snowshoes caused their disbandment. (Courtesy of the Photograph Collection, Public Archives of Nova Scotia, Notman Collection, #66169.)

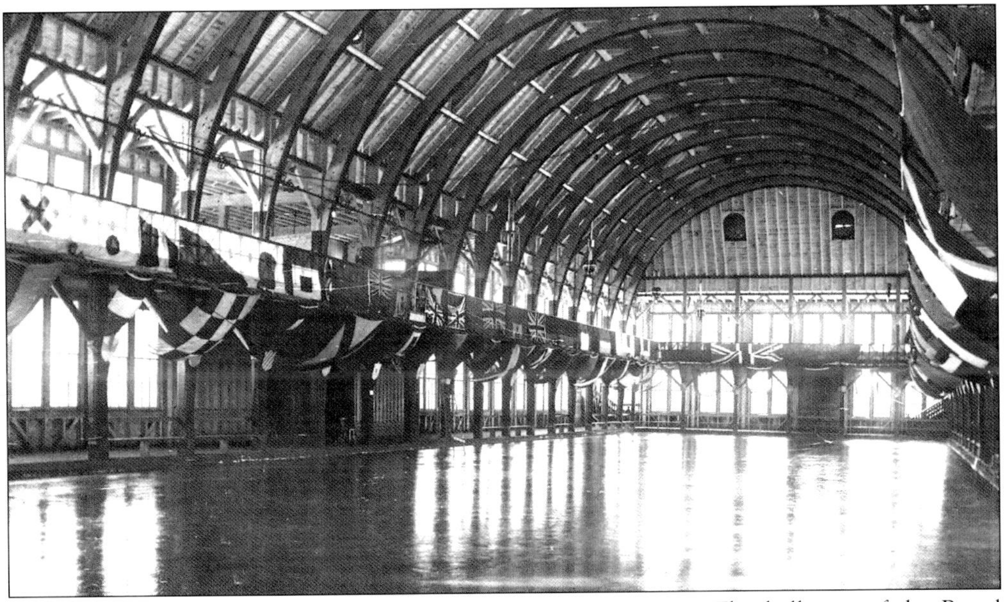

Skating was one of the most popular activities in the Province. The ballroom of the Royal Exhibition Building on Tower Road is seen here *c.* 1885 decorated for an ice carnival. The first ice surface was produced in this building in 1880. (Courtesy of the Photograph Collection, Public Archives of Nova Scotia, Notman Collection, #5115.)

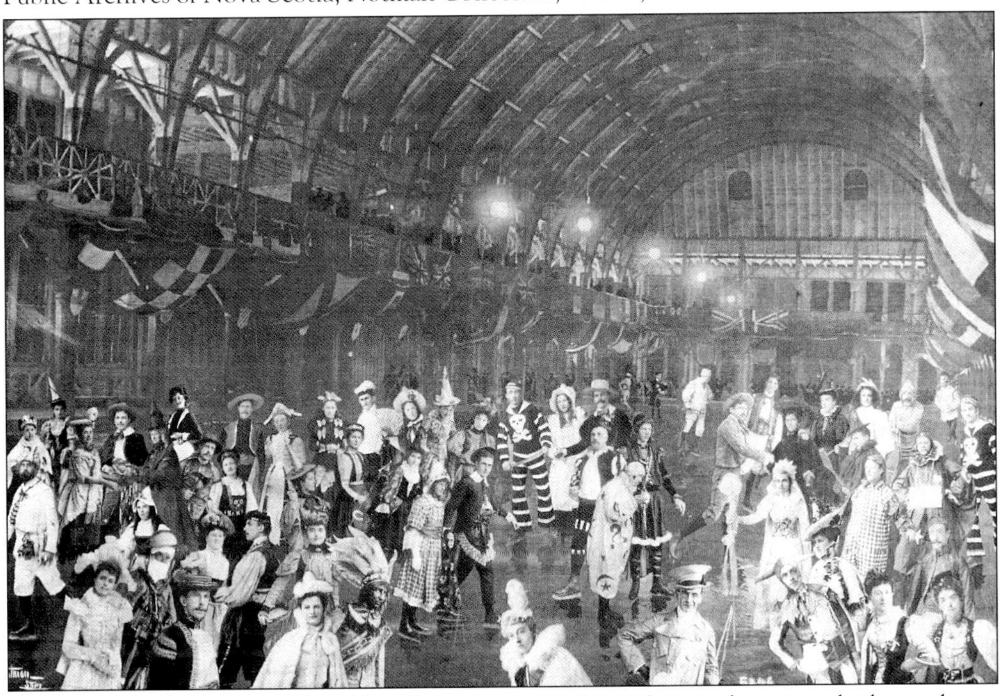

Here, we see the ice carnival itself, with its patrons in fancy dress and wearing the latest skates. In the 1860s, John Forbes of Dartmouth invented the Acme spring skates, which clamped metal blades to the toe and heel of the skating boot. The first covered rink in Canada opened in 1863 on the part of the Commons now occupied by the Public Gardens. (Courtesy of the Photograph Collection, Public Archives of Nova Scotia, Notman Collection, #5246.)

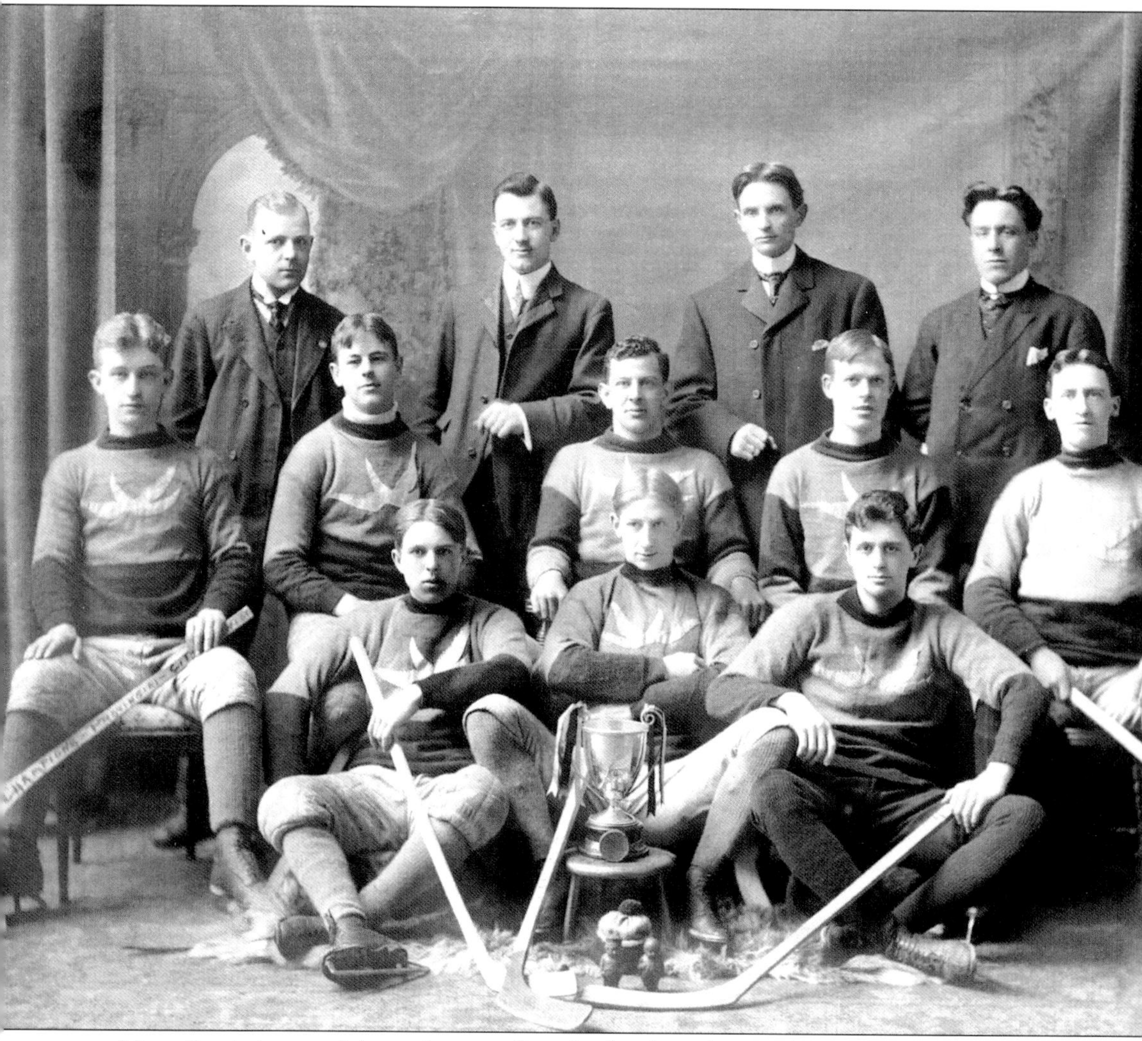

Nova Scotia is one of three places in Canada that lays claim to having been the first venue for the sport. All three have valid claims. Halifax's first account of something similar to hockey, called Wicket, appeared in the *Novascotian* of February 24, 1831. In the 1880s, a league formed in Halifax, with the Wanderers Club, Dalhousie College, Dartmouth Chebuctos, and Dartmouth Knockabouts competing. This picture shows the Crescent Intermediate Hockey Team of 1907. (Courtesy of the Photograph Collection, Public Archives of Nova Scotia, Gauvin & Gentzell Collection, #31, #36-5.)